THE CMO'S
SOCIAL MEDIA
HANDBOOK

A Step-By-Step Guide for Leading Marketing Teams in the Social Media World

PETER FRIEDMAN

LiveWorld
4340 Stevens Creek Blvd., #101
San Jose, CA 95129, United States
marketing@liveworld.com
www.liveworld.com

Design by Andrew Hahn, Verso6
Illustrations by Jonathan Brown
© Copyright 2016, LiveWorld

Ordering information:

Special discounts are available on quantity purchases by corporations, associations, and others. For details, contact LiveWorld at the email address above.

The CMO's Social Media Handbook/Peter Friedman. —2nd ed.

ISBN 978-0-692-21303-2

The CMO's
Social Media Handbook

A Step-by-Step Guide for Leading Marketing Teams
in the Social Media World

Peter Friedman

For my parents, Arthur and Cynthia Friedman,
who taught me the
value and power of relationships

TABLE OF CONTENTS

Chapter 4: Socialize the Brand 41

When marketing = the integration of brand and culture in the service of a human experience.

Chapter 5: Social Brand Identity Planning in Practice 51

See how the process worked to launch one company's first social media party.

Chapter 6: How to Become the Starbucks of Social Media 65

Social content planning requires brands to pour their heart into every post.

Chapter 7: Master the Art of Social Storytelling 79

Harness the power of social storytelling to get more attention, more engagement, and deeper customer relationships.

Chapter 8: Turning the Social Minefield into Opportunity 91

Socialized brands don't just survive social media crises, they use them to build improved customer relationships.

Chapter 9: Legal and Regulatory Issues, Oh My! 109

The dynamic free-for-all of social media understandably makes lawyers nervous. This chapter lays out the issues so that you can make informed decisions and mitigate risk.

Acknowledgments

I have many people to thank. First, my parents, Arthur and Cynthia Friedman, who inspired and supported me to always do what I thought was right, to pursue my passions, to be kind, and to be creative. Thanks to my sister and brother, Joan and Robert Friedman, for all their support. To my daughter, Amy, and son, Jonathan, who are both forever by my side.

Jenna Woodul, our co-founder and Chief Community Officer, not only has contributed to the content of the book, but more than anyone I know understands, lives, and breathes social media experiences. She is the heart of our company. Mark Williams and Dawn Lacallade, social strategy leads at LiveWorld, have made many important creative contributions, sharing their expertise and ideas. Jason Liebowitz, our VP of Sales, helped add punch to the cartoons. Sara Grace, my editorial partner, has brought not only writing skills but content, insight, and humor to the endeavor.

Thanks to the many collaborators and supporters who have helped make Live-World what it is today. To our co-founder Bernie Bernstein, as well as Chris Christensen, Trev Griffiths, Bruce and Debbie Dembecki, James Isaacs, Page Mailliard, Ken Wirt, and the others that helped us get started and grow. To Winonah Gouda-Bauer, who, at a bleak moment for the company, said, "The employees will come up with the money"—and then wrote the first check herself. Barry Weinman was an early investor and board member who believed in us, stuck by us, and has been a great mentor through it all. Bill Cleary, a board member who joined when the going was tough, has been a creative inspiration and is the one who actually said, "You have to write the book on this" (and a few more books yet to come). Joe Graziano and John Sculley were the first to put their investment money and advice where our mouths were, believing in the vision we shared with them.

From Steve Jobs, I learned that detail counts. Steve taught me to hire people on the edge of greatness and push them over that edge. Ted Leonsis, Alan Patricof, and Howard Schultz have been build-a-company mentors, connectors, and friends.

Sandy the Golden Retriever must be given credit as the first to nod in agreement that we should start LiveWorld. Today, Sierra the Golden Retriever has taken up the mantle, always nodding in agreement that things can be great in this moment and the next one.

A deep thank-you to LiveWorld's clients, who have given us the opportunity to work with them to deepen their customer relationships and transform their businesses. Thanks to Ed Stenning, Stuart Meikle, and the Zoetis team, who have been great to work with and shared their case study success.

If I left anyone else out that should be included, thanks to you as well.

The LiveWorld moderator team's voice and presence are the living expression of our company in the space where we work. Thanks to them and to the entire LiveWorld team past and present. We have proved and continue to prove every day that people can create value together that they could not create alone. Our lasting success is a resounding proof point for the power of social media. I can't wait to see what our next decades bring.

Forward

By Jeff Hayzlett, C-Suite, *Bloomberg TV*

When I came on as the CMO of the Eastman Kodak Company in 2006, I made a lot of changes, but bringing the company into the social era was among the greatest—and the most resisted. People thought I was nuts, especially because I personally was out there tweeting every single day. Plenty of people wished I would just shut up. When I started there, over 40 percent of our Internet mentions were complaints, but that dropped down to 7 percent when we started using social channels to talk and listen to customers directly. I asked our people to get to know them. Solve their problems. Share with them where the company was and what we were up to, including our new social media strategy, which everyone thought should be guarded like some state secret.

I spent a lot of time and energy—too much energy—helping my colleagues understand the value of social as a space where you can build deeper relationships with customers by being transparent and spontaneous, and even have a little fun in the process of being real. I believed then and still do today that in the long run, you can make more money by selling less and helping more. Although we made a lot of progress, fast, it often felt like an uphill battle.

If only I had had this book to share with every marketing employee. Peter Friedman reveals the truths of successful and effective social media to explain how it works and why it works from the inside out. He writes specifically with marketing leaders for large brands in mind, a very rare gift in a sea of generalized books on social media. Armed with knowledge, new social practitioners and old can approach the channel proactively, instead of reactively, which is the reception that most new social programs receive from their organizations, even today.

Peter offers 32 years of experience in the social space, and veteran leaders who use his book to bolster their social knowledge can feel confident that they're getting wisdom that is both cutting edge and high-level enough not to be confused by passing trends. This is the stuff that works.

I know Peter personally, and so I know that his commitment to transformative relationships doesn't stop at social. He truly believes, as I do, that better relationships mean better businesses, better products, and better lives. But social is special in that it allows major brands, for the first time in history, to scale their ability to establish direct and meaningful relationships with customers and grow the brand together.

And it's not just (or even primarily) relationships between the brand and customers that create new value, but the relationships the brand can foster among the customers themselves. Companies that tap that magic are the ones that truly become part of their customers' lives. Peter and his company, LiveWorld, have helped hundreds of the world's best-known companies get there, and now the basic blueprint of his strategy is available to anyone smart and lucky enough to read this book. Don't waste another minute that you could be spending getting closer to your customers—start reading, and changing, today.

Introduction

What my father taught me about social media
(before it was invented).

My passion for creating powerful collaborative relationships—essential to leading our company as the founder and CEO and intrinsic to the success of our social media solutions—started with what I learned from watching my father.

For generations, my family had a large printing and publishing company in New York City, where my father was the head of sales and engineering, a very unusual combination. The presses were two stories high and the length of a building, with giant rolls of paper. When I was a teenager, the plant foreman handed me a can of thinner and had me walk inside those presses and clean ink off the rollers. Though I could have done without the cleaning work, I loved being in the depths of those great machines, which produced everything from income tax forms to customized diaries.

Dad always had the view that the best success comes from good collaborative relationships. Moreover, he believed that you should treat people well simply because it's the right thing to do. A great side effect is that doing so often comes back around to benefit you as well. In my dad's 50s, he broke away from the family business to start a new printing company. As head of engineering for years, he had developed and patented many new designs for printing presses and bindery machines. My father had often worked in cooperation with two manufacturers of these multimillion-dollar machines, creating value together, for both his company and theirs. When he started his new company, they were excited to be able to work with him on it.

But then the start-up capital he was counting on didn't come through. He reached out to the two companies, one in England, the other in Germany, and let them know the new business wasn't happening. They both responded quickly, with a similar message: "We've had a collaborative relationship with you for many years. We believe in what you're doing and trust you to make it a success. We'll advance you the machinery you need, and when you're up and running, you can pay us back."

Their contribution was the equivalent of tens of millions of dollars of credit in today's terms, and it enabled my father to start a thriving new concern at an age when many others plot their retirement. In his 60s he started yet another company. Mom helped too. Today, both over 90, they continue to run their business together as a team. As they say, it's not work when you love it.

Fast-forward to my own career. In the early 1990s at Apple, I was chosen to head up the company's first online services division because I had a background in networks and communications. But I could see right away that data running through networks wasn't the only, or even the most important, factor required to make these new online community environments successful. On my first day I met the team and said, "Our executive team thinks this new online environment is all about network pipes. I see it as a new media form, and the degree to which it's successful is going to be the degree to which it helps people socialize and connect to create value through relationships."

Our team grew Apple's worldwide online community (or *social network* in today's terms) to 50,000 dealers, user group leaders, institutional customers, and employees; helped give birth to Salon; and created Apple's eWorld, a clean, well-lit online community space whose strong user culture was stewarded by a team of moderators. eWorld was a critical success but for a variety of reasons didn't make it in the numbers game. In late 1995, Apple leaders told me in confidence that eWorld and our division would be shut down.

For years I had been thinking about starting my own online services company, but I had been hesitant to make the leap. Here was the push I needed. As the clock ticked on eWorld, I put together a fairly conservative 12-page business plan that had me fundraising until June of 1996, then finishing a prototype in December.

In February the news about eWorld closing went public. The moderators who made it such a terrific environment got news that they would soon be let go. As word got around that co-founder Jenna Woodul and I were starting a new, as-yet-unfunded company, we started getting emails from them: "We want to make what you're doing successful. We believe in you, and we'll work for you for six months for free to help you get launched if it will keep this community going."

We set the conservative business plan aside and launched a consumer community website not much more than a month later, with a committed volunteer staff of 70 moderators from around the world and help from about 30 other people who had worked with us at Apple. We had not met even half the moderators in person, but we and our many informal partners were bound together by this idea that online social spaces empower individuals to connect, form relationships, and create value together that they could not create by themselves.

We called the community website Talk City and the company LiveWorld, where I am still Chairman and CEO today and Jenna is still our Executive Vice President and Chief Community Officer. Like my father, I founded a company not thanks to piles of cash, but instead thanks to the trust and value of collaborative relationships.

LLiveWorld has changed significantly over the years. Today we provide conversation management SaaS software as well as strategy, engagement, moderation, and insight solutions on the greater social web and for messaging apps. But we're still in the business of creating value for our clients through the transformative power of online di- alogue and relationships. We're still committed to helping people create more value together than they could alone.

I recently went down to Miami to an annual summit of global chief marketing officers. Working with these CMOs and aspiring CMOs, I was impressed. They all believed in the value of social media-enabled, long-term, engaged relationships with customers to produce a rich value chain: real-time marketing and insight, higher-quality yet lower-cost customer service and support, and long-term revenue growth. Ten, even five years ago, such a group of senior marketing executives would not have looked at the world this way.

But I also heard their frustration in trying to plan and implement social strategy in companies where the business culture wasn't quite there yet. Making things worse, even though they "got it," many of them were marketing veterans without specific backgrounds in social media. That made it difficult to have the confidence and knowledge needed to lead their respective organizations in meaningfully changing the nature of business as usual. They wanted to strategize about and execute social media, essentially a relationship marketing effort, in an environment focused on short-term impulse campaigns. Finally, they felt challenged to define key performance indicators (KPIs) and measure social media, let alone reach an ROI.

I wrote this book to help address that knowledge gap. I want to give you exactly the information you need to take real ownership of your social strategy and program. "The success or failure of [digital] programs ultimately relies on organization and leadership, rather than technology considerations," as the lion's share of 850 C-level executives told McKinsey in a 2013 survey.

CEOs and company teams are looking to CMOs for that leadership. "It's... critical to have the right CMO in place to drive digital programs," wrote Glen Manchester on CMO.com, referring to the McKinsey survey. "These individuals hold an 'outside-in' perspective due to their finger resting squarely on the pulse of the customer experience at all times." An IBM survey in 2013 also noted the trend in leading marketers becoming the official brand stewards company-wide.

In short, it's a terrific time to be a CMO—if you're prepared to leverage social media and messaging effectively in your marketing, customer service, and overall customer experience.   Over time, communicate its power and make change across your entire organization.

This book is part Social Media Theory and Practice 101 crash course, and part practical toolkit, all from a CMO's perspective, to help you with everything from dealing with vendors and establishing your social brand identity, to managing crucial conversations with the CEO, the social media intern, and everyone in between.

I have worked with clients operating in businesses with massive cultural and institutional bias against social—including even major regulatory hurdles that they're powerless to change—who have still created big wins from their social media marketing. You can start small, and build. Showing results is how you start building consensus around broader cultural and organizational change.

Together, let's get your company and customers thriving in social media so that you can create more value working together with your teams and your customers than any of them ever could create alone.

—Peter Friedman
New York City
May 2016

Chapter I:

The Social CMO

Defining the role of the CMO and the new shape of marketing in the social media world.

The days are long gone when marketing could be reduced to "the guys who make the ads." The modern CMO isn't thinking about ad spots so much as *marketechture,* the delicate engineering of the myriad ways a company orchestrates the integrated customer experience across products, marketing communications, channels, and employees. Social media is the opportunity to integrate all these pieces into a consistent, persistent brand experience for your customers.

Social media is the tool that allows you to hear, drive, and leverage the customer's voice at a greater scale than ever before, and then, in the best of cases, help the company and the product *become* that voice. Ultimately this process will reorganize your entire company around the customer, an orientation that will soon be required for a company to compete. For now, if anyone asks you who in the organization owns social media, look him or her in the eye and say, "Our customers." What you're saying is true: effective social media is by, for, and about the customer. If anyone asks who your social media agency of record is, say, "We are."

Marketing doesn't have to completely *own* social, but it should *lead* social on behalf of your company. It may be only the marketing department that's thinking about social right now. It may even be only *you* who's thinking about social. But that's going to change, quickly. Social media ultimately will play a role in how each division develops strategy and makes decisions. In fact, for social to be truly successful, for your company to survive and thrive in the social era, every part of the business must be involved.

Even at that point, there will still need to be someone who takes leadership responsibility on behalf of the entire company. And that person is the CMO.

The Social CMO is the executive who, on behalf of the C-suite, the company, and the customers, leads the organization in creating a social experience that delivers value to customers and in turn helps meet business goals.

Creating that experience doesn't happen at a desk, or in a spreadsheet, or on a whiteboard. It's an experience that is ideally defined and developed at every stage through dialogue among and with the customers themselves.

The 1,000 Year History of Social Media Marketing

"Sir, if you want me to connect engagement to sales,
I'm going to need a better abacus."

That's why the Social CMO is singularly focused on the customer's voice—creating the relationships and the dialogue to hear, understand, and leverage that voice at incredible scale, for a stronger, better, more competitive company.

You Already Know How Social Works

In a general sense, any seasoned marketer knows how to "do" social. It's relationship marketing, carried out in a social landscape. Don't let unfamiliarity with the different channels (Facebook, Twitter, etc.) and the technology throw you off. You already know intimately how this works because you've already experienced it when thinking about the life cycle of customer relationships.

Think about how you leverage the traditional media landscape. You know the fundamentals of reach versus depth: Some channels have very high volume, good for reach but not for deep engagement. Then you get narrower and narrower channels where you can align positioning more carefully. Finally the curve pops up a little bit at the end, where the superenthusiasts create some disproportionate volume and value.

Media Landscape: Reach vs. Depth

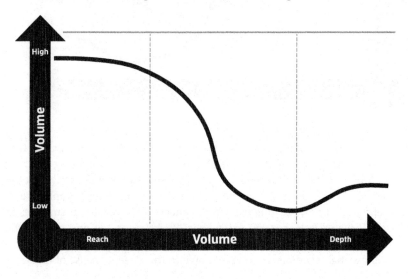

Let's look at TV first as an example. When you advertise on the giant broadcast networks, you get great reach but little depth. "We are now going to interrupt our customer's viewing experience in the hope that this 30-second ad will come to mind when he or she is at the supermarket," goes the thinking.

7

Cable networks tend to reach a tighter niche. It's the same people, but reorganized into vertical markets—Lifetime has a largely female audience, ESPN is for sports enthusiasts, Nickelodeon is for kids, and on and on. You can target an audience better and align your messaging to resonate with that vertical context and the customer's associated frame of mind at the time.

Media Landscape: Television

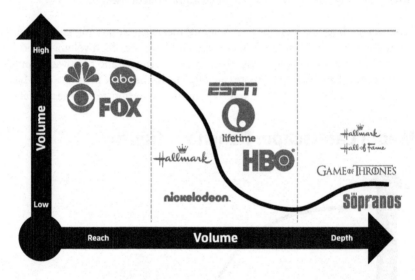

And then you're working on a level even deeper when you've got a show that not only appeals to a specific vertical but also has a real cult following—a show like The Sopranos or more recently, Game of Thrones. Here, fans take on the show as part of their identity, dressing their profiles in the show's graphics, acting out character roles, creating fan art, or otherwise immersing themselves in the story. These experiences can extend the lifecycle of a fan and expand the audience. A brand that associates itself with customers' social self-immersion in these shows has a shot at working its way into their deeper sense of identity.

Media Landscape: Retail

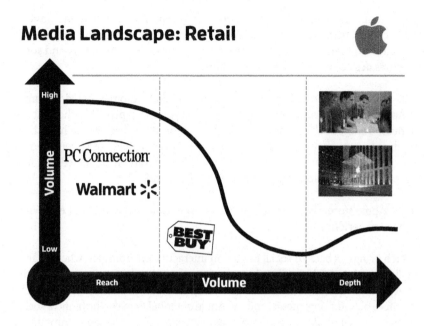

To get the absolute, three-dimensional, *emotional* Apple experience, where do people go? To Apple stores. Here the design, outside and in, breathes the Apple brand. In my days at Apple, we'd sometimes think of the company not as a computer business, but as the most vertically integrated design company in the world. From the machines to the software to the circuit boards, we put design first. The stores have brought that integration forward as precisely and in as emotionally focused a way as have the products.

More than the building exterior, the glass staircases, and the wood counters, it's actually the people in the stores that create the experience. The Apple "geniuses" are the anchor points. (And to use Apple as a metaphor for social media, think of the geniuses as the equivalent of social media's community managers, or brand personalities.) They provide leadership and a point of reference.

But, as in social media, the geniuses don't constitute the most powerful dynamic at work in establishing culture. That role, when properly orchestrated, belongs to the other people like you and me—the customers.

The experience feels like this: You walk in and look around. Set against the backdrop of wood, beautiful Apple machines, and glowing light, everyone seems cool. And if everyone is cool for being there, then so are you. We are all cool Apple people together! It makes people feel good about themselves; it makes them want to come back and bring their friends. People literally put visiting the Apple store with friends on their social agenda. The Apple stores in New York City and some other cities are actually on the tourist maps.

Years ago when we'd talk about this Apple cultural-customer brand dynamic, only Apple people seemed to understand. Everyone else probably thought we were nuts. Today, as the most valuable company in the world, Apple has a brilliant advantage in that many more people are Apple people, and even the rest surely recognize the cultural-customer dynamic the brand has created and fosters every day in thousands of stores around the world.

In the Apple store, shopping isn't a transaction. It's a people-focused emotional and social experience.

Which brings us back to social media, an interactive environment where brands can talk to customers both directly and one-to-many, and customers can do the same, with the brand and with each other. Here, I'd argue, you have both the reach-depth curve of traditional media, and the Apple potential to make the brand a social, emotional, and cultural experience by building deep, tightly aligned communities. Take a look at the chart below, and then I'll explain in more detail.

Media Landscape: Social Media

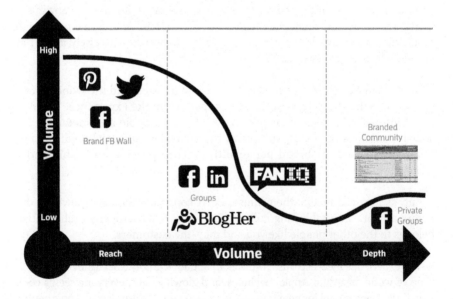

High reach, low alignment:

Branded public pages on social channels like Facebook give brands broad reach similar to that offered by broadcast TV, but without much depth to start. Such channels are terrific conduits to build brand reputation, acquire new prospects, distribute content, and promote products.

Less reach, more alignment:

Here you have segmented verticals on social platforms, as well as partnerships with other social brands on the web. For example, a brand might sponsor a series of posts or a contest on the site BlogHer if its female audience matches the brand's targets.

Lowest reach, highest alignment:

This configuration is the "Apple store" of social. The die-hard fans can be served in private communities, via targeted efforts, or in narrowly focused groups on broad networks (such as Facebook) or on branded community sites. These approaches may serve a subset of customers that is small, but extremely valuable if they become lifelong customers and enthusiastic ambassadors for your brand across the web, on their social networks, and in their real lives.

There is one very significant difference between the social media landscape and the traditional media landscape. The social media landscape is much more fluid, in part because your customers are moving through it organically in real time, and in part because the stages of the curve are more dynamic. In the social media landscape you can go deeper at any stage of the curve, or make any channel work for you at any level of the curve, depending on how you execute.

Social Media Defined

For our purposes here, let's define *social media* as an experiential media form that connects people through online dialogue to create potentially transformative relationships. It's a tool that allows individuals to improve their lives by interacting with groups—both with people and with brands—facilitated by online platforms that erase typical boundaries of time and space.

In the context of marketing, don't think of social media as another channel that merely complements your efforts in traditional media. Instead, think of it as the platform and context for the entire customer experience, and in turn the entire marketing mix. More and more, it will be the primary way your customers experience your brand, and the venue through which you establish and manage your relationships. It's more influential than any other type of marketing, any other channel, and in most cases even the products themselves. This is because when people experience your brand through effectively managed social media, it's a deep people-to-people emotional experience that they'll spend more time on and go deeper with than anything else.

Social can serve many purposes, from distributing content and building a reputation (lowest engagement); to customer service and support (more engagement, plus utility); to building loyal brand ambassadors who in turn evangelize other customers to both experience your company and eventually buy your products (highest alignment, with lasting emotional pull).

To see how a brand can get the most value, first we must understand two critical aspects of how to be social: customer benefits and conversational dynamics.

The true benefits people get from their experience in social are not coupons, or your content, or even product reviews, as so many surveys have suggested. Such surveys have looked only at the situational output behaviors and ignored the underlying drivers of social media behavior.

Customer Benefits of Social Media

The following are primary, *primal* benefits people get from social media that drive them to use it:

1. Self-expression and sharing oneself

2. Making and connecting with friends

3. Getting attention

These are very powerful, fundamental emotional needs people have, which is why they can be so impactful for your brand. These needs also have formed the underlying dynamics of relationship marketing for centuries.

The language I've used to describe social media's primary benefits is consumer oriented, but it is easily reconceived for business-to-business marketers:

1. Exchanging information and expertise; collaboration

2. Networking with other professionals

3. Improving one's standing with colleagues and management

A truly successful social media program provides users with one, two, or all three of these benefits. Yes, you can have a program without these and distribute a lot of coupons, but you could do that with direct mail and tabs as well. If you are not providing at least one of the benefits just listed, you simply are not leveraging the true power of social media.

By the way, to date many social media programs don't provide these benefits. Those programs are not truly social. They are traditional advertising, PR, and digital marketing efforts shoved through social channels, generally talking *at* customers instead of fostering dialogue *among* and *with* them. Which brings us to the second critical aspect.

Conversational Dynamics of Social

Social media is about people connecting with each other through dialogue and in turn forming relationships. A very good litmus test to see if your brand is being social is whether or not your program is encouraging conversations among and with your customers—in other words, generating new connections and a whole bunch of dialogue between customers, not just responses to your posts. This is how we build relationships and affect how customers think and feel.

It's not that every status update or tweet needs to hit this high bar. And in fact, many customers love to read and respond to your content, even content that's specifically product oriented. Why wouldn't you want to facilitate that? But the greatest power of social isn't talking at people, or even one-on-one dialogue. It is creating a space where people get value from access to each other; where they get to express themselves, make friends, and get attention.

A few quick examples. Oreo fans get to share photos of their Oreo experiences, tied to brand-inspired themes. Cooking enthusiasts on the recipe site Epicurious share their secrets to perfect chicken soup. Zoetis Equine customers share incredible photos and stories about their horses. (Zoetis is a LiveWorld client that I'll introduce you to in more detail later.)

These brands use simple posts that help create a sense of social connection, and also offer practical information to help connect followers to others in the brand's social space and sometimes even offline.

Unleashing relationships through social isn't actually that hard. It just requires that you be thoughtful about the needs of and potential connections between your customers, and that you constantly look for opportunities to serve them in ways that complement your brand.

When social media is done well, the customer's experience in that space tends to dominate his or her experience of the brand. Yes, more than even the product itself. It's a place in which a customer's brand experience can become direct, immediate, emotional, communal, and sustainable, because it's more deeply integrated into his or her daily life. This is where engagement lies and unlocks all those benefits that you hear about but that may sometimes seem elusive—brand advocacy and lifetime loyalty being chief among them.

Social in Action: American Express Open Forum

American Express Open Forum is the company's community for small business owners. What drives the community isn't the card or the various ways it helps ease the challenges of business. Customers come so they can connect with other small businesses and learn what they're doing to become more successful. That strikes deeper than just any credit card ever could. Indeed, membership has its privileges—the other members.

Your Defining Mission

As you read this book and look to apply the specific principles, stories, and advice in the context of your business, I want to give you one top-level mission that rides above it all, the same mission that inspired me to work in this field and launch this company.

It's this: Help customers create more value together than they could by themselves. Help your teams do the same. Facilitate dialogue online, guiding your customers and teams toward many meaningful relationships. In turn, customers will think about your company more, feel positive about you, and want to engage with you and buy your products.

Yes, this is all in service of your brand, and there's a lot of value that comes specifically from your brand—the products themselves, social-delivered service and support, the content, and the applications and tools you may provide. But the only potentially *infinite* source of value comes from the customers themselves, and what they have to offer each other. The more ways you can find to tap that, the more successful everything you do in social will be.

So even if you're starting with the basics, keep these questions in your back pocket: *How can I use social to build and leverage dialogue and relationships? How can I make the individual's life better thanks to the interaction of the whole?*

Creating value from community, whether emotional or practical, isn't the only goal of social, but it's where the greatest marketing wins derive. That's where your brand comes to life, guided by your team and animated by your customers.

Chapter I Key Takeaways:

✓ The CMO needs to take leadership responsibility for social media on behalf of the entire organization.

✓ Social media is defined as an experiential media form that connects people through online dialogue to create potentially transformative relationships.

✓ Social media is best thought of as the context and platform for all your marketing, not as just another channel.

✓ Social media follows the same rules as fundamental relationship marketing does.

✓ The three primary customer benefits of social media are self-expression and sharing oneself; making and connecting with friends; and getting attention.

✓ Social media is most effective when customers are talking to each other, not just responding to the brand.

✓ Social media creates opportunities to connect customers emotionally to each other and in turn to your brand.

Chapter 2:

Going Social Starts with a Social Team

Identifying, hiring, and managing the key players on your social media team.

Creating quality dialogue and relationships in social starts with an effective social media team. To get started with that team you need a dedicated social media manager—not a half-timer, not a few people pitching in. You need to start with one full-time social media person. Social is its own set of channels, requiring someone with a skilled background who can give his or her full focus. Add to the team as soon as you are ready—but start with at least one person who is fully dedicated to building relationships with customers through social. That's the bare minimum of what's needed to start and sustain conversations that matter.

Once you've got that person, start small, with just one or two social channels that are a good match for your business objectives. Show some results, and use them to lobby to get that person a dedicated budget. From there, you build slowly, incrementally, always with realistic goals that directly correlate with your company's business objectives. Some of our clients, who represent the largest brands in the world and the most successful brands in social media, started this way.

In this chapter I'll explain why and how to build an optimal team—and who should be on it—whether you're working with mostly in-house resources, mostly vendors, or a combination of both. The goal is a team that maximizes personal, real-time connection with customers and doesn't fall apart when dealing with massive scale.

Dealing with Vendors

Very few large companies have the internal resources or expertise to develop, deploy, and manage social media programs at a large scale, whether that means handling user content volume, deploying a content and engagement model (especially across channels), managing workflow, analyzing the data, or integrating with other marketing efforts. So when it's time to step into social media, their first step is to partner with a vendor.

I can speak to that relationship with experience, because LiveWorld is that vendor partner for many brands. Contrary to some thinking, good vendor partners can learn your voice and help bring it forward with customer engagement. But even if you opt for an end-to-end social vendor who develops and manages your entire program, we recommend that you have in-house people, too. It's not that we don't have our clients' backs. But unlike other marketing disciplines, social goes so deep, becoming the context and platform for all marketing, that having team members who understand the mindset and the medium is extremely important. Your own team members know your company and customers better than any outsider does, and are best situated to help with integration across the organization. Imagine that your social channel is your company's party for customers. You, as the host, can't just hire people to have the party for you. You need to be in attendance. One of our Fortune 50 clients told us, "I get it, but I don't have people. I have money. I need you to be our internal people as well." In his case, we agreed to do it, but insisted on having at least a half headcount on it and that our person have a desk at the company so she could be truly embedded. And it worked.

There's a lot of demand right now for social media marketing support—and so the market has given rise to many solutions and players. Some of them are good, a few are great. Many are not so good. (That's polite for "Don't go there.") So many have hung out a shingle and declared themselves experts in social media, from individuals to platform companies to the largest marketing agencies in the world.

Many companies, worried about consistency, think they should work with an agency that handles all aspects of their marketing: TV, print, digital, PR, and social concurrently. These agencies pitch their integrated model hard. The problem is that it's difficult for one firm to be great at everything. Further, traditional agencies have a built-in cultural bias toward traditional media. You end up compromising "best of class" in favor of convenience. The better choice is finding solutions that allow execution to be optimized for each media form.

And in the social media age, "traditional" now includes digital. For example, an agency might be famous for writing great copy, but it might do it with a broadcast mindset and therefore fail in social. Or a digital agency's forte might be great websites and interactive content, but it might not really understand how to create dialogue and community among customers. Some traditional agencies are so busy making wonderful graphics that the work actually gets in the way of customers talking to each other.

And yes, you need consistency of ideas across your marketing mix. Strong leadership by the brand itself is required to integrate the best-of-class approach. It's up to you to make sure vendors are collaborating effectively. You'll need to make sure that, for example, the guys you hire to build content and manage dialogue on Facebook aren't confusing customers by releasing product messaging that's different from what your digital agency created for your website. Again, you don't want the same content on TV, print, digital, PR, and social. But you want the same *idea* translated effectively to the context of each channel, which usually means not just different content, but a different approach.

How to Get the Most out of Your Vendors

When evaluating potential social media vendors, look for a firm with deep experience in the medium. You'd think that would go without saying, but somehow in this business new and hot compete all too well against firms with a real track record. (And yes, I tilt toward "experience counts," as the leader of a company with experience in social media and online community that goes back 30 years.)

Ask specific questions to evaluate a firm's experience: "With whom have you worked, and for how long?" "What social programs have you developed, with what results?" Remember, generalized marketing experience isn't what you're concerned about here—you're looking for a team with a specific track record of launching and managing social media programs, sleeves rolled up, handling the constantly changing dynamics in real time, ideally with documented ROI. Finally, ask the firm to speak to a track record of collaborative relationships with other marketing partners.

Once you've hired a vendor, think of the relationship as a partnership. You're not "farming it out." No firm can provide "silver bullet" solutions that solve problems while you sleep. Good strategy will require your participation. Look for a partner that's willing to teach your people to fish.

You also want your vendor partner to recognize and respect that your people "know stuff," even if they're not yet experts on social. First, your people know your company and your customers. Second, they know marketing. Third, you may well have social media–savvy people on staff. Social media is about creating value through dialogue and relationships, so make sure your vendor is good at doing that with your *team* as well as with your customers.

A word, too, about expectations as you move forward in the relationship with your vendor. Whatever strategy you develop at the outset, recognize that it will evolve and change as customers respond and interact. That's part of the process of working in a dynamic, collaborative medium. Course correction is a sign that your partner is doing things *right,* not wrong. By recognizing that, you'll give your partner the necessary leeway to leverage unexpected opportunities. As long as you are constantly clear on what your business goals are, you'll have a reference point to anchor you as implementation changes on the fly.

Don't Let Technology Define Your Strategy

When considering technology and technology vendors, you'll often find people pushing technology that provides a one-size-fits-all solution—perhaps to a problem you're not even sure you have! It's rare to find one tool that solves all your needs. It's better to accept that up front and plan a strategy involving a portfolio of tools. Expect to change tools regularly as your context and needs change. Most of all, don't start your thinking with someone's technology sales pitch. Start with *business strategy* and *relationship priorities,* and develop a services plan that you know will get the people dynamic right; that's ultimately where you will succeed or fail. Once you've got the plan working, *then* look for the technology or combination of technologies that will complement your strategy and services. Technology doesn't determine your strategy, it supports it.

Some vendors provide just services, some just technology, some both. Any scenario is fine, but dig deep on each element. You don't want to rely on a tech vendor for services when it turns out the services side is just one or two people trying to fulfill all the snazzy promises on the vendor's website.

How to Get the Most out of Young (Socially Savvy) Pups

A few years ago, brand after brand said, "Just find me a 22-year-old who understands all this social media stuff and give it to him or her." Some of those 22-year-olds did great work, but for the most part, as time went on, brands realized that social media smarts didn't replace the need for senior marketing skills, which take years to develop. You need both to succeed.

The natural fluency of millennials in all things social doesn't mean they should be running your social media marketing program. I watched a number of companies install newly minted grads in senior-level social media positions, particularly around

2009–2011, and saw it backfire about as many times. These kids generally knew very little about social media *marketing*, and still less about marketing in general. Why was anyone surprised that this turned out to be a huge disadvantage?

Generation Social

"I've been on Facebook since junior high—that's years of experience.
Tell me more about the VP position."

As I've said before, your customers will experience your brand through social media more than through any other marketing venue, including the product itself. At the same time, a new social media program is more likely to ruffle feathers in an organization than anything else a CMO could do. Do you really want a 22-year-old responsible for something so fundamental to your success and your company's? No, you want someone with some leadership chops who understands the very real stakes of doing business and representing a brand.

Social in Action: Lego's Social Test

In 2004, the Lego Group nearly went bankrupt. A decade later the internationally loved toy maker is thriving, overtaking Hasbro as the second-largest toy company in the world. The strategy that turned the company around? Putting creative control in the hands of fans.

Social media has been a key part of that turnaround since 2011, when the company hired Lars Silberbauer to develop its social strategy. In May 2011, the company announced its Facebook page, which it took over from a fan who had launched it in 2008. In December 2011, it welcomed kids 13 and over into Rebrick.com, a community site where members share and write about their own Lego creations. The company's social campaigns are focused on fan-driven content that shows the creativity of Lego products and makes an emotional connection to the brand.

Lego's social success has more behind it than passionate fans, great campaigns, or agency partners. Silberbauer also deployed an organizational strategy within Lego.

He believed that for the company to succeed in the social era, senior managers across the company, not just in marketing, needed to have the experience of connecting to customers in social.

Silberbauer's early social campaigns engaged fans immediately, and he took their feedback to corporate management to make the case that business could be transformed if that immediate connection to fans were to go deeper into the organization than the marketing department. As a result, the company integrated social media into its development program.

At *Marketing* magazine's Social Brands conference in London in 2013, Silberbauer explained that Lego's senior managers are required to take a daylong training in social media. When the day is over, they have a written test and then a practical one: they have to post a status update to the company's Facebook page.

"You see the nervousness around the room when they see they need to communicate with customers," said Silberbauer. "But when they get 500 Likes, that's when they realize what social media's all about."

Fortunately, as social media has become ubiquitous and budgets have grown, it has become easier to find and hire people who have both marketing experience and social fluency. The new grads and interns have an important role as well, in increasing the social media savvy of your marketing team, and across your organization. These kids don't "embrace" social media, they live and breathe it. In fact, within the next five years, companies that haven't gone social will have trouble attracting the best and brightest of this young cohort.

Bring these young pups in as part of the team. Leverage their energy and enthusiasm. Right away, pair them with your seasoned people and give them time to mentor each other. Making it clear that each has something to offer the other helps ease defensiveness and close the generational divide.

All marketing people—not just those who touch social directly—need to start to live in the media form your customers are using. Would you let somebody run your TV advertising who had never watched television? Hold formal classes for senior and midlevel managers in social, with the junior folks as teaching assistants. Natural affinity for social media doesn't necessarily qualify you to develop a curriculum to teach it, but work with what you have.

Become the Change You Want to See

Guess what? "All marketing people" includes you. What you've learned about interacting in social by watching over your kid's shoulder isn't enough. Pick the channel that appeals to you and get active on it. This doesn't mean your usage needs to be daily or highly public, although a blog or a public Twitter account can be a great leadership tool. Find a way to use social media that actually works for you, whether that means becoming an expert on LinkedIn or creating an Instagram feed full of pictures of your dog. (I have a Golden Retriever who has several social media outlets.)

What real experts of social media quickly learn is how to manage it, rather than letting it manage them. I've had periods when I've been a real Twitter junkie. I found myself waking up at 5:00 a.m. and spending 45 minutes on Twitter. Then I'd do it again at 8:00 a.m. For every hour of reading, tweeting, and retweeting, I created another hour of follow-up for myself. Finally I had to back off. Now I've found a better balance by using Twitter for live events like trade shows, and sticking to Facebook, Instagram, and the occasional blog post for my regular social interaction. Experimentation is the best way to find what suits your personal rhythms. Find what works and run with it.

Leading Organizational Change

For social media to gain a foothold at a company, it needs a dedicated hub. That means a budget and individuals (whether internal or through vendors) who are accountable to social-specific goals.

Sometimes mandates are needed to make change happen. It's up to you, as the CMO, to declare that it can and will be done. Put a stake in the ground by announcing that all marketing proposals are required to have a social media component. Pepsi mandated this; meetings sometimes ended very abruptly when proposals failed to include social. Unilever mandated that social spend be a certain amount of every budget.

One of our CMO clients has a single slide with the four pillars of the company's marketing. Social is always one of the pillars. All other media forms are subsets of one of the other pillars, but not pillars on their own. This CMO understands the sweeping change that social entails. With this one slide he signals that he knows it and leads his team to embrace it.

You'll generally find that senior executives very quickly understand the need to embrace social. Young hires just out of school do too; if anything, they're frustrated that you're *not* doing it. It's those in the middle of the hierarchy who resist the changeover. These are the veterans who are invested in older media forms, and who often are being judged on related metrics. It's hard for them to shift their focus to anything new when their performance is tied up in, say, advertising impressions.

Most marketing departments have decades of traditional media inertia and cultural cues to support that inertia. Awards are given out for a great ad or a launched website. Social media, in contrast, is less about one-shot glitter and more about building long-term customer relationships and, in turn, sustained business impact.

It's up to you to celebrate social pioneers by building metrics that reward innovation toward social solutions. Celebrate those who invest themselves. Status and recognition are most important. Bonuses are good too.

With time, incentives, and proven results, the social hub you started with will develop spokes, as people in multiple areas of the organization take on social and interface with that central group.

Never Forget That Social Isn't an End, It's a Means

Social media is the tool that allows you to become truly customer driven. Conversation leads to involvement. Involvement leads to deeper relationships and customer commitment, which lead to sales. Conversation also drives better insight. Better insight means better marketing, products, and experiences for your customers—and more revenue and profit for you. True customer-centricity means that social media can't stop at marketing. The customer closes the loop by giving feedback (whether purposefully or incidentally) that can and must affect everything from marketing to sales to service to the features of the product itself.

Your goal is to set the paradigm that customer insights are taken seriously and, when appropriate, pushed to action. Of course, you're the CMO, not the CEO. You don't control everything. (And in our new social media world, neither does the CEO. The customer does.) Nevertheless, there are steps you can take to move things in that direction. For example, when I was at Apple, and later when working with eBay, my team gathered customer feedback gleaned from social media each week, then presented the top 10 trends weekly to the C-suite for discussion.

Do this, and let everyone in the company know you are doing this. First, it brings your execs closer to your customers and drives important and better decisions. Second, it's a practice that sends a clear message: this is a company that cares about customers, listens to customers, and acts on their feedback. When the rank and file see those at the top behaving this way, they are inspired to do the same.

Bringing Employees Under the Tent

Over time, if you're making progress, many—maybe even most—employees in functions far beyond marketing will be interacting with customers through social channels. Every employee is a potential brand representative, which has incredible tangible and intangible benefits.

Many senior leaders looking to engage employees in social face cultural and institutional hurdles. Companies have traditionally dealt with employees and information flow using a command and control model, with hard rules and low levels of trust and individual agency. Empowering employees to represent the brand in social means loosening the reins. Instead of imposing hard rules and compliance checks, leaders must build a strong company culture in which employees are mutually committed to a shared set of values and prerogatives. Employees are provided with guidelines and training, and then trusted to engage directly and spontaneously with customers.

For example, at my own company we have taken explicit steps to build a culture that empowers employees. We began the process by developing a shared understanding of our overall goals and values. One of the principles I learned while working with Steve Jobs was, as he put it, "to find people on the edge of greatness and push them over the edge." At LiveWorld, we have extended this concept. We find *groups* of people on the edge of greatness and push them over that edge, together. We do that internally, and we do that for customers. Social media is a team sport. With that concept as our foundation, we have developed core principles that help employees step up to the plate as active, empowered thinkers and representatives of our brand. Your company needs its own cultural foundation.

Sure, unleashing employees in social carries risk. But the rewards are real: Employees are empowered and engaged more closely with the brand than ever before. They also get to know the customer more deeply, improving their ability to make decisions focused on customer needs. Only when employees are at the center of your social program does total customer-centricity become achievable.

Chapter 2 Key Takeaways:

- ✓ A social program should start with at least one full-time social media manager and goals that are tied to business objectives.

- ✓ Both vendor partners and in-house team members are valuable in scaling up a social program.

- ✓ In selecting and collaborating with vendors, choose firms that are best of class for social media and in the particular element of social media at hand. Then take an active role in making sure their combined efforts are well integrated within social media and with your other marketing vendors as well.

- ✓ An effective social strategy is supported, not defined, by technology.

- ✓ Social media–savvy millennials have much to offer your social strategy, but they shouldn't be primarily driving its implementation. Pairing them with seasoned professionals allows for mutual mentorship.

- ✓ As CMO, you are in a unique position to reward social media pioneers and expand the social hub.

- ✓ Social media enables individuals at all levels of your company to interact with and gain insight from customers.

Chapter 3:

Of Course You Can Measure Social ROI

Those who say that social media ROI can't be measured are completely wrong.

There's nothing I'm more passionate about than helping brands develop a social culture that amplifies the customer's voice, opening an authentic, generous dialogue that makes everyone better in the process. But because we're all in business here, I'm going to discuss ROI first. Your success as a CMO—and the size of your budget—will often be determined by your ability to show ROI.

It's a myth that you can't measure the ROI of social media programs, I'm happy to say. You can—and not just social media metrics ROI. You can and you should have real business ROI.

As with any media form, there is a range of ROI types, from ROI based on metrics of the media form itself, to marketing, support, insight, and even sales ROI. And as with any new media form, these are all developing in real time. For all its growth and penetration, social media marketing is still in its early stages. It has quite a bit more growth to come, and we are still learning to apply traditional ROI measures even as we develop marketing formats and associated ROI measurements intrinsic to the context of this new channel. Edward Stening, the Senior Manager of Digital Strategy and Multichannel Marketing for our client Zoetis, shared the frustration of many social marketers in satisfying management's expectations for ROI.

"Not being able to tie social directly to sales is a constant battle. I couldn't do this with TV or billboard or print five years ago. But they somehow think we can do it with social," he told us. "With digital, we can be more refined, and obtain solid metrics about the purchase cycle and how close we can get to it, but ultimately if I'm not selling direct, there's a lag; it goes from person to person to person and possibly through other steps [in our channel]. If customers see a TV ad, we don't see that sale the next day. There's a process."

In 2013, 38 percent of $1 billion–plus consumer companies reported a positive return on their social media investment in a survey conducted by Tata Consultancy Services. Meanwhile, 44 percent of companies surveyed reported that they had no "methods in place" to measure ROI, and 18 percent reported negative social ROI.

From my own experience, I expect that the companies that have trouble demonstrating ROI from their social programs fall into two camps: those that weren't strategic in connecting business goals to social implementation up front, and others that, for a variety of reasons, failed to measure the results of their time and effort.

Challenges with and confusion about measuring the return on investment in marketing and keeping pace with the times are a very old story. Marketing leaders struggled in the past to demonstrate the ROI of billboards, television, public relations, digital, and Internet channels, to name just a few established tools without a direct connection to the revenue they drive. Social media is just the new kid on the block, and we're still in the process of developing industry-accepted proxies to measure value and impact.

Think about TV ads. Toward the end of the 20th century, controlled testing models correlated television reach statistics (gross rating points) with sales. An underlying premise was that a short TV ad—which itself evolved into a kind of mini–TV show—would grab the audience's attention and motivate them to make a purchase. That was great for the first few decades of TV, when it was the primary media form garnering consumer attention.

But that's no longer the case. TV watchers generally have their primary attention on a second screen, a phone or tablet where, more often than not, they're engaging in social networking. And after 60 years of 60-second ad spots, audience members are now looking to their peers, through social media, to influence their purchasing decisions. And yet these same 20th-century models for measuring television ads are still in use. There's nothing wrong with using reach to help measure sales ROI, but the model needs updating, especially for traditional media.

To develop the same level of credibility for social stats, all that's needed is to run comparable controlled studies and A/B testing with customers touched by a social program and not, so that you can look at how a program aided awareness, intent to buy, and purchase. A marketing department that knows how to quantify results from more traditional outreach should be able to apply those same skills to look at social media. (It seems this department sits at a different end of the building from the social media marketing people, but so it goes for all new media forms.)

Of course, you can't wait for those people to do those studies, so let's take a look at the range of ROI measures you can use in social media today, and seek to understand them specifically in the context of this specific media form. I'm going to work loosely from least to most powerful in terms of meaningful business impact.

I. Social Media Statistics ROI

Social media comes with many stats options, from the social networks themselves and from all sorts of analytics packages. There will be no shortage of trackable data. The challenge is to make meaningful use of the metrics. Let's take a look at some of the main stats.

Five Social Media ROI Models

ROI Model	Returns
Social media statistics	Fans, Likes, engagement
Marketing statistics	Reach and awareness, marketing equivalency
Learning	Insight
Relationship building	Customer support ROI, loyalty, word of mouth, advocacy
Sales	Intent to buy and actual purchase
Short term	Impulse actions that lead to name acquisition or single purchases
Long term	Sustained revenue growth over time

Fan count metrics: Currently called page *Likes* on Facebook and *followers* on Twitter, these numbers tell you how many people have signed up to be connected to your social media presence. Building your customer audience is important, of course, but just building these numbers in themselves yields a vanity metric.

29

Lots of fans and limited engagement doesn't usually meet business goals. If you build a big fan base with impulse tactics, such as coupons, those customers aren't likely to pay attention to you beyond getting their deal. On Facebook, 95 percent of the people who Like your page will never come back to it. They don't see your content on your page, they see it when it shows up in their newsfeed. If you want to keep reaching them, you have to build content, create conversational dynamics, and deploy targeted ads that will make their way through Facebook's algorithms and human social behavior to get to the fan's newsfeed. Facebook ads have evolved from traditional Internet banner formats to content story formats. So here again, your ads need to create social interaction to succeed. The one-way traditional ad model won't get you far in this channel.

Engagement metrics: A much better measure of social success, engagement metrics track your fans' interactions with your content and each other. Such metrics come in a variety of forms, vary across channels, and are always changing as the industry develops. They include *retweets, Likes, shares, talking abouts,* and *comments,* to name a current few. For these metrics, consider that the more involved the action is, the more the customer is thinking about and feeling connected to your brand, and the greater his or her commitment to your social experience. The greater the commitment, the more likely it is that this person is spreading the word to others and making purchases. Liking a comment is good. Sharing or retweeting it takes more effort and is a statement that the user thinks the comment is worth the attention of others. Commenting is the best, because that takes more energy and time and suggests the person is truly engaged, mind and hopefully heart. This person is sharing his or her social presence with you, and acknowledging that you have done the same with him or her.

Engagement, you'll find, is often fleeting. Your newest followers tend to engage more than those who Liked you a year or even a month ago. This is why it's so important to create content that users care about—which is usually content about *them,* not you—and to engage them with ongoing conversation. Tracking individual customer visits and their engagement over time provides a more complete picture.

Engagement metrics can also be deceptive. You can get high numbers only to find that the engagement in question isn't supportive of your business goals. Consider a brand post that recently garnered 2,600 responses. The digital agency, used to thinking in terms of driving web traffic, immediately said, "Great, let's do more posts like this!" But when our team dove into the actual user conversation, we found that 1,600 of those comments were totally off topic. That's not bad in itself, except that off-topic threads often develop into negative conversations. And indeed, 1,300 of those 1,600 comments were negative. So, contrary to the surface metrics view, this wasn't a post that we'd want to repeat at all.

Further analysis of the actual conversation resulted in a change in strategy, which ultimately delivered a 25 percent reduction in negative comments month over month and a 65 percent increase in engagement over several months.

2. Marketing Statistics ROI

In much the same way major consumer brands like Nike or Coca-Cola use advertising to build brand awareness, often with little reference to a product and without any call to action, successful marketers can use social outlets to drive awareness—the shallow end of the reach-depth influence curve from chapter 1.

Companies that focus on brand awareness using reach as their most important social media objective tend to have an easier time with their KPIs than companies that focus on other goals, such as increasing web traffic, sales revenue, or lead quality, according to a 2013 Ascend study. Of course, there's the danger that skeptics will question how valuable that additional reach is to your brand, so think about pairing this goal with a form of marketing that's higher on the value chart, such as lead acquisition.

For example, you might look at how much traffic social drives to your corporate site, or how many people downloaded a white paper that you pushed through a social link. By adding an email capture to the download, you could tie the social promotion of the paper to a lead acquisition KPI. Specific KPIs will be based on your business sales process. Are you trying to collect more email addresses to begin a conversation with potential new customers, for example, or looking to increase the amount of money existing customers spend with you? Identify the goals and measure the results you get using social media, compared to those from using your various other outreach tools; finally, look at the results of combining social media with other outreach tools.

But how do you translate this information to an ROI for your marketing staff and for your CEO? Marketing equivalency ROI neatly solves that problem.

The marketing equivalency approach to ROI is nothing new. It's how public relations agencies have long measured return on investment in media outreach efforts. Using marketing equivalency ROI should reveal how social media costs compare to those of other media, ideally demonstrating that social achieves its goals more efficiently than other spend. I have clients who really like using marketing equivalency because the marketing department has its arms around its own spend, and so can arrive at ROI figures independently.

Determining marketing equivalency ROI is fairly straightforward. Measure your social reach, then ask what you would have to spend to get the same numbers in digital, print, television, and radio with standard CPMs. To get more sophisticated, consider that there's a range of CPMs to assign to different aspects of your reach. For example, some experiences aim for reach that is broad rather than targeted, and call for a low CPM. Some are more targeted, reaching more qualified audiences and thus warranting a higher CPM. Some involve direct customer interaction and conversation, which would translate to a very high CPM—so much so that these experiences can be equivalent to an in-store interaction, which some companies rate at being worth $100 to $400 per visit, or for a very high-end sports car, $2,000 per visit.

Suppose a specific social media program runs $300,000 to reach 2 million people with 600 million impressions. Factoring in a range of appropriate CPMs, you might calculate that it would cost $4 million to get the same results through advertising.

Once you calculate a campaign's marketing equivalency ROI, you can go to your CEO and say, "Instead of spending $4 million on traditional marketing on that campaign, let's spend $300,000 doing it through social channels, save a few million, and increase our overall social media budget!"

3. Learning ROI

Social creates a giant 24/7 focus group by offering your marketing team (and anyone else you encourage to participate in the channel) real-time connection and conversation among and with customers. What you'll find is that what customers reveal when they talk to each other is even more authentic and useful than what they tell you directly. The real-time thoughts of people discussing your brand produce valuable quantitative and qualitative data—though exactly what that value is may be hard to quantify. The opinions they express there are apt to be more honest and less self-conscious than what they would have contributed in the structured, paid environment of traditional focus groups. When it comes to quality insight ROI, automated sentiment analysis isn't enough. It requires human eyes. The technology helps a lot, but generally it only can be configured to see what you already knew you wanted to look for. Human eyes are needed to discover what was previously unknown, if the language is nuanced or in an unusual usage pattern.

Searching for insight is much more complicated than measuring content volume. For example, sometimes you might see a trend that's not particularly high volume but very passionate; you could be seeing the canary in the coal mine. The trend could show what might be coming, possibilities not even on your radar yet, and it's important to listen.

Edward Stening of Zoetis spoke to the value of social as a market research channel. "[Our social marketers] know what customers like, they know what they don't like, what pisses them off, they know how to get a reaction from them. They know what brand messages will or won't excite them, what time of year to talk with them," Stening said. "It used to be random; we'd send out a mailing, do a print ad and a TV ad, and we'd get research nine months after the fact. At the moment our marketers can get on our social pages and can learn more about their customers from a half an hour of looking through our engagement than what they would have learned from a market research document. We've tried to use this as a keyhole into the world of the customer."

Ken Winell, former digital evangelist of the New York Road Runners, now in the same role at Doublespace, offers a great, high-profile example of social media being leveraged for real-time decision making. His team used social to help decide whether to go forward with the 2012 New York Marathon amidst the incredible damage and destruction of Superstorm Sandy.

Social Media Sizzle Stats

25%
Increased profits from reducing customer churn *(Leading on the Edge of Chaos, 2012)*

42
Average number of people social customers tell about a good customer support experience

53
Average number of people social customers tell about a bad customer support experience *(American Express, 2012)*

$16 million
Extra sales from a 1% increase in word of mouth *(Cisco, 2009)*

$49 million
Extra sales from a 1% reduction in bad word of mouth *(Cisco, 2009)*

21%
Revenue lift from customers who have a good customer support experience *(American Express, 2012)*

"There was a groundswell of commentary, both for and against running the event. We had to relay information to the management team to provide up-to-the-minute feedback. We measured sentiment and tried to give management 'word clouds' with the phrases people were talking about, showing them the river of news that indicated the big picture of what people are talking about. The next piece is giving them positive or negative sentiment, so they can understand it like a 'traffic light' orientation where green-light people are feeling positive, or red-light people are negative on a subject," Winell told marketing technology strategist Howard Greenstein.

"It is important to leverage social media as a listening post. In one form, it's an extension of customer care, and in another form, it is giving you product feedback and suggestions. If you're engaged with customers, having a dialogue and an ongoing community, you'll learn who the posters and the leaders are, and you can start to influence them. You can create calls to action and drive behavior," said Winell.

4. Relationship-Building ROI

Here you're getting into the deepest potential ROI: enhanced customer relationships, which ultimately become sustainable sales ROI. Relationship-building ROI stats include increased customer loyalty, brand advocacy, and intent to buy. Loyalty and intent to buy can be measured by interviewing customers, with A/B control groups and before-and-after social media involvement. Brand advocacy can be measured by flagging (a.k.a. "tagging") comments or content attributes and listening for customer reviews or mentions of the brand across the social web.

One of the most recognized paths to both relationship-building ROI and associated financial impact is customer support delivered through social. Exceptional retail has always been about customers—listening to their needs and wants; really talking with them; and creating great, personalized experiences. Customer service via social media is simply adapting these retail principles to new channels, often improving efficiency in the process.

Cable provider Comcast was a pioneer in social media customer support, with Director of Digital Care Frank Eliason leading the way with his @ComcastCares Twitter account. Before the end of 2008, he'd already handled 22,000 tweets with a simple philosophy: "Can I help?"

Brands that deliver customer service and support through social media also experience big wins in strengthening existing relationships—more relationship-building ROI. The 2012 American Express Global Customer Service Barometer Study showed that two-thirds of customers who have used social customer service say they are willing to spend more with a company that provides excellent service through that channel.

"Delivering outstanding service [through social] creates impassioned advocates and can serve as a powerful marketing weapon for companies," according to Jim Bush, Executive Vice President of American Express World Service, in a company press release. "For example, consumers who have used social media for service in the last year are willing to pay a 21 percent premium at companies that provide great service. They also tell three times as many people about positive service experiences compared to the general population. Ultimately, getting service right with these social media–savvy consumers can help a business grow."

Many companies find that customer service improves when you deliver it in a social forum, because, as they say, "Nobody is as clever as everybody." When our team at Apple deployed online customer service for the company in the 1990s, we found that because Apple's millions of customers used the products a great deal more than Apple could, they helped the company build up an incredible knowledge base of what worked, what didn't, and what to do about it. The customer support community served customers better (and more affordably) than the company could have done by itself—and the incredibly valuable side benefit was that by providing the space for peers to help each other, Apple customers became emotionally linked to the brand. The customer service experience became about much more than tech support.

In case you want to dismiss this as that ol' Apple magic, LiveWorld saw the exact same thing happen with the sellers' community that we helped eBay manage and grow. It was originally created to provide auction support, but it quickly became a social culture, a full-blown online society that sellers lived in. It became a destination not just for technical support, but for support in many aspects of their lives. Ultimately we developed a separate, dedicated area for customer support.

Social customer service delivers high quality for both customers and the brand. It has vast reach and brings in more information from customers, enabling a company to better understand and organize issues, develop resolutions, deploy faster, and adjust. It also costs less. Fully allocated phone support costs can range from $10 all the way to $100 per inquiry, depending on the industry and whether the agents are in the United States or offshore. Email and chat support tends to range from $5 to $10 per inquiry.

Social can lower those costs even further, because service reps can work faster and handle multiple inquiries at once, bringing the cost per inquiry down to $2. And again, customers will often support each other when service is delivered through a social venue. When customers support each other, the marginal cost is $0 per inquiry.

When we first deployed a social support program called Ask & Answer for eBay, it immediately saved millions of dollars per year compared to email support. It took just a few months for the savings to effectively justify eBay's entire online community program.

Through social, you can stay in close contact with customers well ahead of and long after the point of sale, giving you many more opportunities to turn satisfied customers into active brand ambassadors. Finally, you can increase the likelihood that next time they need what you offer, they will start that process with you, not your competitors.

Social in Action: Duane Reade's Parallel Persuasion

Duane Reade made headlines in 2013 when it hit and surpassed 1 million followers on Twitter—a big number for a drugstore chain that only operates in New York City. The company's successful campaigns, such as the "Boo-tiful Legs" campaign, which asked shoppers to photograph themselves in Halloween costumes that featured hosiery purchased at the store, have all been designed with a very specific ROI equation in mind. The company calls it "Parallel Persuasion," defined as Brand Advocacy + Brand Voice + PR Integration + Conversation Relevance = Social ROI.

"This equation has allowed us to be highly visible via social as a regional chain here in the New York Metro Area, nationally and worldwide," Calvin Peters, Duane Reade's PR and digital communications manager, told *Retail TouchPoints.*

The Boo-tiful Legs campaign generated 157.4 million impressions on Twitter alone, using the designated #DRLegCandy campaign hashtag.

BOO-TIFUL LEGS
HALLOWEEN LEG CANDY PHOTO CONTEST

ENTER TO WIN
October 13th to November 3rd

5. Sales ROI

There are two kinds of sales ROI from social media. There's the direct revenue lift brands see when they push promotions through social. This is a hard ROI—but it's limited compared to long-term sales ROI generated from relationship-building ROI when customers become active with the brand community, form a deeper relationship, and build a space for the brand and its products in their and their friends' everyday lives. Here is where we see increased loyalty, increased lifetime customer value, and enhanced revenue growth that's sustained over time.

Of course, the number most CEOs and managers have traditionally wanted to see is immediate sales directly generated by marketing activity. That's a bit of a short-term mindset, pushing messaging at customers to make a quarterly buck, without care for the long-term relationship potential. In any case, for some companies, particularly those with the ability to follow a click from social media through to an e-commerce conversion, direct revenue ROI is an achievable goal. Of course, short-term sales aren't *bad*. They're good—as long as the promotional push to make them happen doesn't compromise building a social experience with committed, long-term customer relationships (and the revenue they create).

If you are going to try to connect social media messaging to sales, you will need to craft your messages with measurement in mind. Post a coupon or coupon code so you can track redemptions, or use a call to action that sends customers to a landing page where you can measure click-throughs and such desired visitor activities as sales inquiries, sign-ups for your e-newsletter, or purchases. Sales can also be measured through controlled A/B testing and customer surveys.

If you have an e-commerce site, you can put links in your social comments and then track click-throughs and resulting sales. One of LiveWorld's clients with this model was able to track several million dollars of sales annually, a fig-ure that was many times greater than the cost of that company's social pro-gram. That was a specific click-through and buy measurement, and didn't even account for the sales resulting from people who were influenced by the social program but came back later to the commerce website through another route, or the sales impact from friendly word of mouth. That same client also received five times the number of visits to its corporate site when it started including so-cial content on it. There are many ways to use social to drive sales directly, some more creative than others.

Many retailers, both online and brick and mortar, are now finding ways to wrap social around a shopping experience, which can enhance both relationship-building and sales ROI. Think back to the dynamics of the TV shopping channel QVC: Hosts there constantly refer to the people calling in, reminding viewers that their shopping experience is shared with others. The act of buying becomes a way to seal a relationship not just with your company, but with friends in the community that exists around your brand. Wet Seal's shopping community, the Runway, provides a great proof point. The Runway is a user-generated virtual closet, available on the website and through an iPhone app, that lets you assem-ble outfits using pieces available on the site. *Forbes* reported that shoppers who use the Runway are 40 percent more likely to buy something and spend 20 per-cent more than shoppers who aren't part of the community. The more a social program *involves* the community, the higher the conversion is apt to be. Here your KPI, as was the case at Wet Seal, could compare dollars spent by customers who participate in social features against dollars spent by those who don't. For a harder ROI figure, you could measure general revenue growth before and after the social features were in place.

Of course, for most companies, the sales process has many touchpoints, making it difficult—but not impossible—to evaluate the sales driven by any one media form. You might need to make some philosophical decisions about how to attribute credit for revenue, along with technological investments to create an interconnected understanding of your customers and their behavior.

Peter R. Sachse, Chief Stores Officer for Macy's, said integration of the retailers' data is essential in regard to both the customer experience and his ability to manage results. "Department stores built all these systems in silos—customer databases, payment databases. So you've got to merge them. And the ultimate holy grail is real-time location-based marketing that is relevant and personal," he told *Think Quarterly.*

Macy's, which has moved enthusiastically into social marketing in the past few years, has seen some direct sales ROI from its online efforts, which wrap social around a traditional e-commerce experience. "The power of e-commerce extends far beyond the keyboard and onto the sales floor," said Macy's CEO Terry Lundgren in his keynote address at the Shop.org Annual Summit. "Every dollar spent online influences $5.77 spent in the store over the next 10 days."

Selling Social ROI to the Organization

When advocating to your top management for your social media program, proven ROI is obviously persuasive. But it isn't the only way to sell social in the organization. At a panel during the 2014 South by Southwest Interactive conference, multiple social media leaders for big brands spoke to the one-two punch of anecdotes supported by data to sell social to skeptical parties.

Rick Wion, McDonald's Director of Social Media, shared a customer care story from the early days of the brand's life on Twitter. A mom at McDonald's tweeted that her kid's Happy Meal had made him cry: They had given him the toy for girls! Now, this was not necessarily a disaster; arguably, it was a teaching moment. But for this parent, on this particular day, it was a worst-case scenario. "That kid's devastated. That parent's day is ruined," said Wion. "We fixed it, and that customer now is a major influencer who's now one of our biggest advocates."

Noha Abdalla, who heads social at Capital One, said that even though the culture there is extremely data driven, anecdotes are persuasive. "When execs ask, 'Well, how do you *know* you're interacting emotionally with customers?' I just show them the tweets," she said

Selling Social in the Organization

"Wait—you mean social media marketing costs money?"

Chapter 3 Key Takeaways:

✓ Your social programs can and should have real business ROI that you can track and share to improve those programs, justify spend, and increase support in the organization.

✓ Social media statistics are generally the least meaningful form of trackable ROI. Relationship-building ROI and sales ROI are the most.

✓ Marketing equivalency ROI is a traditional PR measurement that, applied to social, can help make a clear financial case for social marketing efforts.

✓ Insight ROI provides valuable business intelligence gained from social media conversations.

✓ Sales ROI is much more valuable when it represents the result of relationship building that produces loyal customers who buy more over time. Short-term sales ROI is valuable but can come at the expense of relationship-building ROI when the brand is too promotional in social spaces.

✓ ROI is essential for improving your social programs and demonstrating results to others in the organization, but sharing stories of incredible customer wins through social media offers a powerful complement.

Chapter 4:

Socialize the Brand

When marketing = the integration of brand and culture in the service of a human experience.

With the role of social clarified, and with a commitment to do it right with dedicated focus and resources, it's time to connect your business goals to the social media program. This starts with thinking about what it truly means to take your brand social. Remember, a truly socialized brand has social at its core, establishing the culture that feeds from social into every other touchpoint—ads and broadcast media, partnerships, promotions, retail, direct messaging, events, digital, PR, and the products themselves.

It's up to the company to create the foundation, or *social brand identity*, that attracts, guides, and helps build a dynamic social experience that's aligned with the brand's values and goals.

To see how that works and why it's important, consider Oreo and its famous spur-of-the-moment tweet during the power outage at Super Bowl 2013: "You can still dunk in the dark." Clever, to the tune of 15,000-plus retweets and almost 20,000 Facebook Likes during the first hours. Ultimately that single tweet won 525 million earned media *impressions*. The press was still talking about it days later, giving Oreo even more eyeballs and attention. Ad critics called it "super smart" and "brilliant and bold." Oreo won the Super Bowl ad competition with a free tweet, up against hundreds of millions of dollars in produced TV spots.

But Oreo's success wasn't just about being quick on the uptake. The "investment" that led to the tweet's viral spread was more than the few minutes it took for the company's agency, 360i, to conceive of, approve, and post the tweet and its accompanying image.

In fact, the cookie company had spent years taking its already iconic brand and using social media to create an experiential culture in which millions of engaged followers participate. Oreo knew its audience well enough (culture) to crack the right joke. And that audience was (and is) an attentive, enthusiastic community aligned with the brand's social sensibility; when audience members saw a great tweet, they passed it on immediately to their own followers. Oreo has successfully created a broad network of loyal brand advocates, people who love Oreos—or even just the idea of Oreos—and experience the brand as more than a product.

To put it another way, Oreo has *socialized its brand* by weaving a positive social experience and particular culture into everything it does. When the Super Bowl opportunity came along, the social brand identity to leverage it was already in place.

Taking Social Brand Identity from 2-D to 3-D

Earlier we talked about the geniuses of real-world social brand identity, the folks at Apple. In fact, all the best retail merchants already know what it means to create the social architecture to some degree, because they've inevitably fine-tuned their retail store to create a particular experience. The collection of items offered; the type of space and store layout; the lighting; the music that's playing; and, most important, the way the service team dresses and interacts with customers—all these things come together to create an experience for the customer, who then takes on an identity as a shopper. You see the same thing in restaurants. The underlying culinary ingredients aren't all that different from place to place. The uniqueness lies in how the restaurant creates the entire experience that brings customers back again and again. The menu is part of that, of course, but so is the decor, the music, and how the waiters dress and engage the customers. All the elements combine to give diners an experience with each other that both suits and supports the restaurant's identity. (And when done right, that experience is the best way to make the cuisine itself shine.)

These days, with social media at the fore, the single most important element of a customer's experience—in-store or online—is becoming the social element. How are all the elements of "architecture" coming together to help people connect with your representatives and with each other in a shared culture around your brand?

Social brand identity guides the relationships you have with customers, the relationships they have with each other, the content you share, and the interactions and conversations you create and inspire. The color and style of the background or chosen channel may add some ambiance to your virtual space, but the conversations and content are what define the experience.

The key dynamic to understand is that your customers will assume that the experience they have with your brand in social media is the experience they will have with your brand elsewhere: in-store, with customer service, through the products, and so on. If you do great for them in social, they'll believe you'll do great for them elsewhere. Conversely, when you fail them in social, why would

Social in Action: Social Brand Identity Blooper

One quick-service restaurant we worked with experienced the harm that's caused when a brand fails to build a consistent social architecture. This company's targeted in-store experience was family friendly, including lots of kids and teens. Its social media presence should have matched that same target sensibility. The company was working with a very edgy ad agency known for creating provocative content. The agency created award-winning TV commercials that were edgy for the brand, but short lived in the mind of the viewer and therefore not a problem. But when the ad agency, fairly new to social marketing, took that same content and used it to create conversations on the company's Facebook page, things went immediately awry. The agency asked fans, "How would you like your meat today?" and trolling teenagers were only too happy to answer. They flooded the company's Facebook page with lewd responses. Suddenly the on-page experience wasn't the family-friendly dinner party atmosphere the company wanted to project and create in its restaurants.

they think you'd do better elsewhere? The social media experience should be—and *will be,* in the customer's mind—akin to the in-store or product experience.

Getting Clear on Goals

Connecting with customers as a socialized brand doesn't start with a magic Super Bowl tweet, or any tweet. It starts with planning. We like to call this strategic planning process the Social Brand Identity Program. Depending on its particulars, a company might go through the process once for its overall presence, or go through it many times for specific brands or audiences. The resulting brief directs the social media program and informs the rest of the marketing mix about the strategic context for social. Here I'll provide an overview of how the process works.

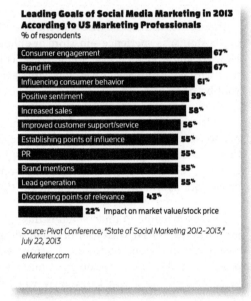

Leading Goals of Social Media Marketing in 2013 According to US Marketing Professionals
% of respondents

Consumer engagement	67%
Brand lift	67%
Influencing consumer behavior	61%
Positive sentiment	59%
Increased sales	58%
Improved customer support/service	56%
Establishing points of influence	55%
PR	55%
Brand mentions	55%
Lead generation	55%
Discovering points of relevance	43%
Impact on market value/stock price	22%

Source: Pivot Conference, "State of Social Marketing 2012–2013," July 22, 2013

eMarketer.com

The Social Brand Identity Program starts with a social audit in which you evaluate what's going on with your brand, with your competitors, and in your industry around social media. Next is the extremely important process of linking established business goals to social implementation, and to specific potential KPIs.

Without goals established up front, even the most ambitious social program is the ill-defined equivalent of flailing your arms at customers. Social is a terrific business opportunity—if you treat it as one. There have been several high-profile stories about big brands spending millions on social media but failing to see results and therefore shifting back to traditional media. What you find when you peel back the layers of the onion is that these situations don't usually represent a failure of the medium, but a failure in the planning and, in turn, the execution. Your goals don't just inform what and when you will post to social media—and what you will *not* post—they point to what you will measure to see if it's working.

Business goals often come down to "selling more of our stuff." But, as we've seen in chapter 3, social can also aid other goals, such as brand awareness, positioning, education, increasing loyalty, improving customer support, lowering costs, or gaining insight.

To start identifying appropriate goals for your company, take a look at where social media has benefit for your business, set goals, and build relevant KPIs from there as you develop your social program.

Finding the Brand's Social Identity

Once goals and targets are established, the rest of the Social Brand Identity Program is concerned with socializing the brand. That process has three parts:

1. **Develop a socialized brand identity and culture:** Your company is entering the social media conversation so that you can better relate to customers. But companies don't connect; *people* do. Which means that to project and enhance your brand in that space, you'll need to conceive of the brand as a *relationship dynamic.* If the brand had a human avatar, how would that avatar interact with customers? What would he or she bring to the relationships you establish in social? Taking that a step further, how will you create a sense of place, context, and ambiance that uniquely brings the brand alive as a three-dimensional experience for customers in social media? The metaphor of a party is again appropriate here: Is the experience like a sit-down dinner? A post–PTA meeting gathering? A chic soirée? What kind of party you'll throw depends on your goals, your socialized brand statement, your target audience, and of course the broader brand values and attributes you'd like to bring forward.

2. **Determine brand participation:** Practically speaking, now that you've developed the *persona* of your socialized brand, how is the brand going to participate in social media? Who will be its voice? What assets and content will it contribute? How will you bring employees into the conversation? How can social media let customers peek behind the curtain so that your company is no longer an entity, but a living, breathing collaboration of people delivering your product?

3. **Integrate across the marketing mix:** Integration means incorporating your social campaigns into your TV and print ads, packaging, web presence, events, and sales process, and vice versa. It involves not just listing your Facebook URL, but giving people a glimpse of the activity there, maybe featuring user content. Over time, social media will ideally be foundational to the entire marketing and sales funnel—that's the truly socialized brand.

Prepare to Give Up Control

The Social Brand Identity Program gives your company the blueprint it needs to socialize the brand. But don't engrave that blueprint on a stone tablet, because the process of socialization can't in fact be completed internally. It requires *customers* to help you explore and redefine the relationship, and with it, your brand.

Today, the job of social media marketing teams isn't just to rack up followers, but to engage customers to form real, loyal, sustainable relationships. A socialized brand doesn't create one-way, top-down relationships. Your team will need to find ways to share the creative process with customers, and make the customers the most vivid brand personalities on your pages.

You are all inevitably familiar with the Dove Campaign for Real Beauty. Most of the press written about the campaign has focused either on its enormous success or on the inevitable controversy that comes when people—especially those in the cosmetics and self-care industry—discuss beauty and body image and the supersized role they play in women's lives.

Few talk about what was truly revolutionary in the campaign. It reaches back to its very beginning, when the company first launched ads featuring "normal"-looking women rather than typical model types, and invited customers to speak out on its social forums (which LiveWorld built, managed, and moderated) about their own experiences of "real beauty." Women did, enthusiastically, posting stories that celebrated inner beauty without being constrained by Madison Avenue's ideals. They also shared challenging issues—and were comforted to read similar stories from thousands of others. During particularly active months, the average number of posts per day was 25 to 28 posts per user!

The campaign turned the entire cosmetics industry on its head. That industry's advertising stock and trade had always focused on pushing images of unattainable beauty on customers. That's the last 60 years' mass-marketing model of the brand controlling the message and the content. Never before had such a campaign been driven from the customer's point of view rather than the brand's. *That's* what made the Dove campaign the gold standard for successful social media marketing, and I believe it explains Dove's resulting gain in market share in countries around the world.

Beyond sharing their personal experiences, customers couldn't stop talking about what was now their favorite brand and line of products. Dove, in fact, was highly sensitive about the product talk, wanting to keep the campaign message-focused and not compromised by commercialism. But the customers wouldn't have it. Having been given a space to be understood and to connect and converse with other like-minded women, they were determined to reward the brand that empowered them with word-of-mouth recommendations and purchases. Our moderators let the conversation build organically while encouraging deeper levels of conversation.

This is the aspect of social media that is most difficult for marketers and companies to accept: the need to give up control, to share the brand development and the messaging around it with the customer. This is where the greatest advantage lies.

Today Dove is no longer just a beauty-products brand, or even the company that celebrates natural beauty. The brand has become a lightning rod for debate on sensitive issues affecting customers, and in turn the industry that serves them. And more important, it is a safe place for women to engage and share their experiences with other women.

Engagement is what's required for customers not just to interact with your content, but to truly advocate for you as a result of their connections with each other, and to do so across the social web—on Instagram, on product review sites, on their Facebook and their Twitter, via email, and on their blogs. The Internet is a big place, actually infinite, and if you want customers loyal enough to help you cover it with brand-positive dialogue, your marketing (and indeed your entire company, but let's start in your own backyard) needs to enlist them as trusted partners. You need to inspire them to imagine alongside you, building the brand through their own experiences and dialogue, so they're not just engaged but *involved.*

If this sounds ambitious to you, that's OK. You can start taking steps in the direction of involving customers. For example, ask your customers what they want from your brand, and specifically what they want from their social experience. Create a poll with some options while inviting their own ideas. You can incent them with prizes, but in a successful social environment, recognition is a far more powerful incentive than cash. Why? Because recognition hits one of those three fundamental customer benefits discussed in chapter 1: getting attention. You can't bask in the glow of cash, but you can delight in others knowing you made a contribution great enough to be featured on a brand's page. Asking for feedback sounds simple, but so few companies do this, and few among those that do really act on the feedback they get. They're too focused on top-down, brand-centric broadcasting strategies.

Marketing folks are highly creative people who typically have great ideas and enthusiasm around figuring out how best to communicate them. Customers, meanwhile, generally have strong feelings around what they want and what's important and interesting to them. They don't want content that's slick and professional, they want content that moves them because it's funny or it's true. It's reality TV (starring them or individuals like them, "the other people in the Apple store") versus a slick, scripted TV series. The easiest way to get there is to involve them in the creation. Even reality TV is produced, so we're not talking about a free-for-all. If you can get the real-life customers and the marketers working collaboratively, the creative potential is endless.

Social in Action: Co-Creation for the Win

One of the most fully realized (and wildly successful) examples of co-creation I've ever been involved with remains Sprint-Suave's In the Motherhood (2007–2009) campaign. LiveWorld was the social media partner providing strategy, technology, moderation, and engagement. Together, the brands built an online community for young moms, had them submit their real-life stories, and then chose the best to produce as story lines for a web series called *In the Motherhood*, cast with professional actresses. A social media experience (in this case, in the form of highly popular discussion forums) was wrapped around the programming. This web series, a unique blend of user and professional content, was so popular that it was ultimately picked up by ABC as a network television series. Suave increased its brand share over the course of the campaign, and Mindshare, the company that devised the campaign and produced the web series, won an Effie Award.

Trust and Authenticity

With this level of relationship comes new responsibilities. There's an old saying, "The worst thing for a bad product is a good ad." Well, the worst thing for a hypocritical company is an effective social media presence. Once you've begun a dialogue—which is the intention you're announcing when you set up a social presence—there's no way to get away with faking out, misleading, or lying to customers, or having marketing positioning inconsistent with your products or brand promises. Social will make your company an open book, whether you choose to lead the conversation or not. Even if you choose "not," customers will create their own social forum.

Authenticity and transparency aren't limited to how you respond to critics and crises—in fact, they can't be. Authenticity and the trust it creates have to be built over time, through each and every interaction. Think about Patagonia and Zappos—they're market leaders not just because they offer quality products and services, but because they've defined their mission—or as Zappos CEO Tony Hsieh puts it, their "return on community"—and everything they do supports it. That's real authenticity, and it takes more commitment than getting exactly the right conversational style in your status updates.

Chapter 4 Key Takeaways:

✓ A socialized brand has social at its core, establishing the cultural context in which customers experience the brand through dialogue and relationships.

✓ The social media experience should be—and will be, in the customer's mind—akin to the in-store or product experience.

✓ Social media strategy starts by connecting business goals to social implementation, and to specific potential KPIs.

✓ Your social brand identity follows on your overall brand identity, extending it to establish how customers will experience the brand through dialogue and relationships in the context of social media.

✓ The social brand identity is at the core of an implementation plan that guides and helps build a dynamic social experience for customers.

✓ A socialized brand integrates social messaging across the marketing mix.

✓ The brand's social identity develops as customers participate in social conversations; their dialogue and relationships ultimately define the social experience, and in turn evolve the brand's social identity.

✓ Social media demands total transparency and authenticity.

Chapter 5:
Social Brand Identity Planning in Practice

See how the process worked to launch one company's first social media party.

In the last chapter, I gave you the theory behind social brand identity and the a strategic planning process that creates a blueprint for socializing your brand within the context of clear business goals and your target audience. Now I want to show you how it works on the ground. Zoetis, a long-time LiveWorld client, graciously agreed to serve as our lead example.

Zoetis is the leader in the animal pharmaceuticals market, selling $4.6 billion of medicine a year. Historically, the company had an indirect relationship with its customers because veterinarians prescribe its products. Until 2012, Zoetis had been Pfizer Animal Health (PAH). The company came to us specifically to work on its livestock products, starting with Zoetis Equine.

Together, we created the social brand identity and culture that prepared Zoetis to launch into social. The first "event space" for Zoetis' online party would be a Facebook page called EQStable, for which we developed a comprehensive content plan and media strategy. This was followed by the launch, content posting, moderation, and data analysis—but this chapter focuses on the initial framework building.

The EQStable About page includes this mission statement:

Zoetis Equine is driven by our passion for horses and their well-being, and for the equine industry and those it supports; this is the force behind our Facebook page. The consequences of disease and lameness impact not only the animal but the owner as well. We stand with you to provide you and your veterinarian with the best products to help your horses enjoy long, healthy lives.

Today EQStable hosts a thriving conversation with more than 100,000 members and a phenomenal engagement rate of over 20 percent. Before we talk more about the great results, let's talk about how we got there.

Goals, Objectives, and Measurements

Zoetis was looking to directly engage end customers of its equine products through social media. The intent was to build community, value, and awareness under the new brand and extend its premium sales experience to a wider set of customers than the sales team could reach directly.

Social Brand Identity Framework

- Goals, Objectives, and Measurements
- Target Audience
- Socialized Brand Identity and Culture
- Brand Participation
- Marketing Integration

> ## Together we identified the following goals:
>
> 1. Create a direct dialogue with horse owners
> 2. Reinforce the brand change from PAH to Zoetis
> 3. Extend the premium customer experience

In other words, Zoetis' goals were primarily marketing objectives, with some customer support thrown in via #3.

So our first step was to identify the business objectives, craft specific goals, and then create ways to measure performance with KPIs. The more specific your goal, the easier it is to develop metrics that match. Many new social programs start with social media metrics (Likes, engagement, etc.) as their goal. Those all have value, but we recommend starting with your actual business goals. (This would be an excellent time to review chapter 3 on ROI.)

Often the goal is "sell more stuff." Almost all of our clients would like to do this. Wouldn't you? Then let's see if we can use social media to do it! But to do it right, we have to narrow it down. Which stuff are we selling, and to whom? Is directly driving revenue the only—or even the best—business objective for social?

Your own business objectives most likely fall somewhere within these four categories:

1. **Sales goals:** Short-term revenue lift tied directly to social campaigns and activity

2. **Relationship goals:** Relationship marketing for improved positioning, awareness and education, customer acquisition, or long-term sales generation

3. **Customer service and support goals:** Improving customer satisfaction while lowering the costs of achieving it

4. **Learning goals:** Gathering data and translating it into insights that can guide business decision making

Write down your overall business goals, then take a look at how marketing is supporting those goals. Then consider how social media specifically can contribute, and how you might measure those contributions. Some of the KPIs may not become clear until you get deeper into the implementation process, but you should get in the habit of constantly linking goals to metrics as the plan evolves.

Target Your Audience

So you've got your goals. Now, what target audience is best suited to help you achieve them in social media? Nothing is more influential in driving execution than your target audience.

In the case of Zoetis, the company's end customers are a mix of small and medium producers, family ranches and farms, and individual owners. (Vets are also very important customers and influencers for Zoetis, but this program was focused on engaging the end customer directly.) All three groups were suitable targets for the stated business objectives, but the question we needed to answer was which would be best served with a social media solution.

Business owners—busy, balance sheet–focused, and not particularly active on social media—weren't a great fit, although the company made plans to connect with them via an informational newsletter. Similar with ranchers, for whom a Twitter deployment had potential as a newsfeed of useful information, which would meet their interests.

But what about individual ranchers and their families? They were more likely to be active in social media, plus they were passionate about their animals and excited to share that passion with others. They were a terrific fit for engaging in a direct social dialogue and so became the primary target of Zoetis' first social campaign.

Developing Zoetis' Social Identity

With goals and targets clear, we moved into the culture work: helping Zoetis discover its social brand identity and culture. We started by reviewing the Zoetis general brand identity, and then working with the company to reconceive the brand as a *relationship dynamic.* The goal is to have a deeper, more personal relationship *among* and with customers thanks to the immediacy and directness of the social channels. So what are the dynamics of that relationship? Why would your customer want to "make friends" with you in social? How is the brand relating to its target audience?

This is incredibly important, because it doesn't just define the content that the brand pushes out. It also serves as a model that helps guide and define how fans relate to each other on the page, creating an experience there that in turn draws more customers into the Zoetis social dynamic.

In this stage, the practical focus, values, and overall identity of your company are important guides. But just as important to understanding the relationship dynamic is thinking through who your customers are: demographics, psychographics, behavior profiles. Keep in mind that we're talking about the customers that you're seeking out in social media. Depending on your business, this may be different from, or a subset of, your usual target profile.

We express that relationship dynamic in a *social brand identity statement*, a declarative statement that summarizes everything I outlined earlier. Zoetis' social brand identity statement clearly reflects both the company's and its customers' values:

*We are your **neighbors with country business smarts**...We have a deep understanding of your business and your community, are quick to lend a hand, and can connect you with the solutions you need.*

Questions to Help Develop the Socialized Brand Statement:

- What kind of relationship should your target customer have to your brand: Are you a cool friend? An older sister? A parent? A teacher? The best boss you ever had?
- What's the slogan for your relationship?
- How does the relationship empower and/or entertain those who visit, and their networks?
- What should your customer tell others about the relationship?

Defining the Cultural Model

Next up is determining the cultural model that would best allow that relationship dynamic to flourish. In the Zoetis example, what kind of party would be a natural fit for country neighbors to connect and be social?

After a broad discussion of the brand and its customers, we landed on "Barbecue at the Fair." The brand-led conversation style would be informal and friendly, with community hosts who loved horses and could easily be next-door neighbors.

Here are a few other hypothetical examples:

- Energy drink—paintball excursion

- Bookstore—book group meeting at a café

- Cookie company—creative play among clever friends

- Sexy women's magazine—friends on a road trip

- Clothing retailer with an ever-changing inventory and daily deals—an adventure in shopping

The cultural ambiance you're building doesn't necessarily have to apply only to a niche of your audience. Take Nike, for example. Their most famous slogans—"Just do it" and, more recently, "Find your greatness"—work well on ads targeted at athletes, weekend warriors, and reformed couch potatoes alike. (How would you translate either of those into a social group dynamic?) Likewise, though Zoetis' target audience for its social campaign is private horse owners, the company's socialized brand view works well across the equine customer mix.

Whether your company's social presence is a barbecue, a chic cocktail party, a weekend seminar with golf, or a pajama party, you need to figure out how to build the experience of the party in the social world of websites, pages, brand content, and customer conversations. As with any good party, its success will be due to a combination of the creativity and quality of your planning and preparation, and your skills in orchestrating your guests' experiences organically once they arrive.

Questions to Help Define Your Party Type

- In what kinds of real-world environments would I find my target audience? Where do they like to hang?
- What kind of party would my target audience want to attend?
- Also, what kind of party does it make sense for our socialized brand to throw, given our goals, values, and product? And where do the two overlap?
- What do customers talk about in their social time? What are their shared interests?
- What conversation style fits our socialized brand statement and business goals? How will our customers speak?

In social, this orchestration occurs almost entirely through content, conversation, engagement, and moderation—all of which evolve in real time with the help of insight. If you're successful, customers connect and return because you are providing value by meeting one or more of those primal needs: self-expression and sharing oneself, making and connecting with friends, or getting attention.

But for now, how are you going to tell "guests" what kind of party this is, so that they can feel comfortable and get excited to make connections?

Through...

Conversations driven by text, images, and video: Your status updates and shared content create a context that guides future user-driven conversations. Your content's vernacular and voice should match the feeling you're trying to create. To communicate that voice to team members, create a style guide and a set of example posts. You can also use photos and videos to illustrate the lifestyle you're targeting. Those visual elements will help, but remember that social is not like broadcast, print, or digital media, where high production values drive the emotional experience. Customer conversations (usually text) drive the emotional connections, supported by customers' own visuals (usually photos).

Linkage ideas: These are interest threads, beliefs, or subjects that link your customers to each other, and allow you to take the conversations at your party a level deeper. Through these conversations, customers become connected to your brand, too. Not only have you helped them connect with others, but also you've shown that you understand what matters to them and are truly interested in serving their needs. The old marketing model interrupted what customers cared about in order to deliver brand messaging. The social model flips that, giving you the job of finding ways to continue your customers' *existing conversations* on the things they already care about.

Once you develop a list of linkage ideas, you can use them to drive content development. Think about your target audience: What are they interested in? What are their challenges?

In the case of Zoetis' audience of horse owners and ranchers' families:

Linkage Idea	Supporting Content
Local community	Support local rescue efforts and promote community activities involving horses.
Family values	Invite fans to share stories about the role their horse plays in their family, today or in childhood memories.
Nature and land	Invite fans to share tips and stories about trail riding and camping.
Horses	Saved this for last because it's so obvious.

Content wrapped around these linkage ideas resonates with these customers. It makes them want to be part of the community, contribute to it, and bring in other customers. They see immediately that Zoetis understands where they're coming from and what they care about. They see that the focus of Zoetis' efforts in social is to give back to and represent the customers, not relentless brand promotion. Nobody wants to go to a party where the host just talks about him- or herself. They want a chance to interrelate with the other guests. That's the party they come back to, with friends.

In that context, occasional posts about horse parasites and Zoetis drugs don't feel promotional so much as like helpful information from trustworthy friends who care as much about horses as they do.

Units of social exchange: My co-founder Jenna Woodul coined this term, which establishes the currency or value flowing through the social experience. All cultures have specific models of value that indicate what's important to that culture. Again, consider your target audience. What do they want and need? When they come, what can they share with each other to satisfy that need? Does it align with your business goals?

Zoetis' main unit of exchange is images of and stories about beloved horses. The brand has been very successful in engaging customers in this way. Active customers don't just want to look at other people's pictures, they also want to share their own (primal need: self expression/sharing oneself). By sharing, conversations and goodwill develop readily between customers (primal need: connect with/make friends). And finally, customers can experience satisfaction when their horses get Likes and comments (primal need: attention and recognition).

Social in Action: Recipes as Units of Exchange

Many food companies, health and cooking magazines, and TV shows use recipes as their primary units of exchange in social media—and wisely so. Much like breaking bread together in the real world, sharing recipes and discussing where they come from is a sense-oriented emotional experience that quickly opens the door to friendship and connection among strangers.

Those connections emerge even more readily with the right push from brand moderators. That's what we found when we worked on the community site of a popular soup brand. We asked site moderators not just to share recipes, but to tell stories about times they had served those recipes. They successfully encouraged customers to do the same. Over time the cultural focus of the community became a lively, ongoing discussion of how people used cooking to take care of their family and friends. The brand became an integral part of the daily lives of their customers, who reciprocated by not only buying the products more often but also recommending that other customers do the same.

Engagement and moderation: Quality moderation is where the real-time party hosting comes into play. As Jenna once said, "If you bring people into your house, you don't send them to an empty room and go to the movies. You work the room—introduce them, give them something to do." A social engagement specialist or community manager can draw people out and see what they need—welcome them, orient them, and let them know who else is there. That sense of context helps get people talking. You also need moderators and community managers—think of them as DJs—to keep the conversation on track, ebbing and flowing with the goals and mood of the party.

And just as some parties have bouncers, moderators keep the conversation clean and kick out troublemakers, or "trolls" in social parlance. The goal is to keep your social environment consistent with the values your customers expect. Those values vary by brand, of course. Is yours family oriented or edgy? Businesslike, with the social dynamic of a weekend off-site with golf, or exciting, edge-of-the-seat fun, like a Super Bowl pizza party?

Customer personalities: What better way to show the kind of party you're throwing than to highlight other guests and maybe even share the hosting duties with them? Identifying, cultivating, and spotlighting "superfans" strengthens your community and guides the brand in providing an experience people love.

For example, in 2007 Dell launched a social space called IdeaStorm, where customers could submit ideas and vote on the ideas of others. A frequent contributor over the years was a user named Jervis961, who shared lots of great ideas to fix all the problems he saw with Dell's products and services. Dell didn't shut him down, it embraced him. In 2011, when he had become the top contributor on the site, the company hired him to run it.

As loyal customers emerge, find ways to reward them with recognition and status. Find ways to support them. Often brands jump quickly to the idea of financial incentives. Bonuses and discounts are appreciated by customers, but they're not sufficient to sustain a community of lasting value. Instead, reward loyal customers and positive contributors by giving them attention. Feature their posts on your page. Refer to them in your conversations. Take recognition a step further by putting their content and photos on your store walls, and in your print and TV ads.

Finally, find ways to empower them. Give them official responsibilities, as well as direct access to representatives and job opportunities when they come along. Once you've created strong enough leaders, more often than not, the job of the brand is to follow—to move the party in the direction customers want, provided it's still appropriate for the brand and its goals. As you do that, the relationship gets deeper and real trust starts to emerge, between its members and in the brand.

Brand Participation

In social, your company isn't just the product and brand itself. It's all the people who collaborate in delivering that brand. The more opportunities you can find for the people behind the brand to participate, the easier it is to connect and build relationships in social, and in the long-term to personalize the brand in the eye of the customer.

At Zoetis, we got the entire equine products team involved. Where relationships already existed, staff made specific asks of potential party guests to share the new page. Other times, they reached out cold to introduce themselves and kick off long-term relationships. This approach not only provided seed content but also brought forward the employees of Zoetis and allowed them to embody the host role, as people who are passionate about horses and consider their job a mission to give horses and their owners happy, healthy, and wonderful lives together.

Think about it: Whom do you want to buy stuff from? A faceless corporation, or people who not only reach out to connect but also link you to a community? Otherwise put, people who are friends, or who you sense could be.

Aside from that, getting employees involved in social helps make real-time marketing happen. As Edward Stening of Zoetis has said, "We've got people on our team who are actual customers, for example, horse riders. Some folks ride all weekend and have pictures of horses on their desks. They thought they knew everything about the customer, until we got into social. They've been able to increase their understanding around their market space and their customer."

Many pages have a designated, publicly identified host or hosts charged with representing a particular social channel or channels on a company's behalf. Many brands prefer not to share their brand power with any particular individual, but it can be worthwhile to identify the individuals who lead the management of your sites or social media. This works particularly well if you're looking to have a brand representative who is a true peer of your customers—for example, a new mom for a baby food company or a teacher for a company that markets curriculum materials—and you just don't have that person on your team.

Some brands develop "personas" to help orient visitors and show them that they're connecting to real people, not brand robots. The company Solarwinds, maker of IT management software, shares tips with customers via its "Head Geek," Josh Stephens. He appears in videos, but his red hair and beard made for a great cartoon avatar, too. Your host doesn't even have to be human. The Facebook page of the historic East Village watering hole McSorley's Old Ale House has featured status updates from the establishment's cat Minnie, who was a beloved fixture at the bar until the health department banned her.

Sometimes it makes sense to have an expert, such as a doctor or product specialist, who can answer questions and correct bad information. Zoetis offers tips from vets.

Brand participation doesn't stop there. All of your employees are terrific assets and can make appearances in your content. For example, during Teacher Appreciation Week, Dell shared pictures of employees holding posters that explained how their own teachers had inspired them, while encouraging similar stories from customers. How can you connect employees to the cares and concerns of your customers so that they can mix it up at the same party?

Questions to Ask to Personalize the Brand

- Who will act as hosts at our social media party?
- How can employees be featured in content or otherwise participate?
- How can we let customers get a behind-the-scenes look at how we make our product happen?
- How can we demonstrate that our employee culture has a unique voice?
- What assets and existing content do we have that could help us show that our brand is unique?

Integrate Social Across Marketing

Social media isn't an "if you build it, they will come" medium. Very rarely does a brand's new social platform initially expand to a large audience organically. Usually a page needs advertising and promotion to launch. There are exceptions: the odd viral miracle or maybe pages that are part of an active cultural franchise, such as a Disney movie. Once you've attracted and engaged an audience, their activity can create organic growth—but the extent of that growth will depend on the depth of the culture you've created. Your social media campaign will find traction more easily if it becomes part of the larger marketing mix, from ad spots to product packaging.

When Zoetis kicked off its first social outpost, the EQStable Facebook page, the company featured the new site on its corporate home page and in its marketing communication during the launch period. We also made sure that employees added the new URL to their email signatures.

Integration means featuring your social campaigns and platforms in your TV and print ads, web presence, events, and sales process. Don't just list your Facebook URL; give people a glimpse of the activity there by featuring user content. (Bonus: When you do that, you're strengthening the existing community by giving social media users marquee attention.) Ask provocative questions, include community member answers, and direct customers to where they can join the debate. Integrate your social media presence directly into the product where you can. For example, include customer tips with a cosmetics or computer product. Let your employees be members of and evangelists for the community.

Integration, particularly with traditional advertising, can prove challenging, as it forces marketers to shift from a "broadcast at the customers" approach to a customer-driven dialogue. Sixty years of TV and mass media have elevated the commercial to an art form and created an industry with an auteur mentality that favors big budgets and slick production over authenticity and co-creation; that favors awards for great one-shot creation (an ad, a website) over sustained relationship building.

Questions to Ask When Integrating Social

- Are social content and links available on company websites and on product packaging? In print and TV ads?
- Is the socialized brand experience consistent in other customer touchpoints: ads, in-store experiences, customer service, packaging, etc.?
- How can our social team start to seed and collaborate with traditional marketing?

Zoetis' Awesome Results

Let's look at how the brand measured the success of its first social implementation against each of the original goals after launch.

Goal #1—Create a direct dialogue with horse owners

The page launched in January 2013. In about a month it attracted over 107,000 fans. The program developed a phenomenal 29 percent engagement rate within the first two months—more than triple the average ratio for communities of pages this size among the top 1,000 brands on Facebook.

The page's visibility in members' newsfeeds is high, thanks to a good balance of brand content and highly engaging social content.

Other key metrics, two months post-launch:

- EQStable fans had posted 13,469 comments to the page and created 333,687 stories, creating a high degree of visibility within their networks.

- Community members actively ask and answer questions.

- Member posts were 97% positive.

- Member posts were less than 1% reportable.

- Hundreds of downloads of a parallel mobile app resulted.

On the relationship ROI side, Zoetis was able to build its new end-customer name list for a fraction of the price of the next most cost-effective method the company used.

Goal #2—Reinforce the brand change from PAH.

- EQStable is generating 5% of "Zoetis" mentions on the Internet.

Goal #3—Extend the premium customer experience.

- There is extended brand engagement, with 15,000+ interactions.

- Many customers self-source content and images (400+).

- High-quality wellness content has demonstrated value to fans, as measured via surveys, activities, and sentiments expressed in comments.

The company is so pleased with the page's success that we are working with them to create social media programs for some of its other product lines.

Chapter 6:

How to Become the Starbucks of Social Media

Social content planning requires brands to pour their heart into every post.

I ended the last chapter by sharing the breakthrough results Zoetis experienced after launching its social media page. The company needed first to create the strategic framework to socialize its brand before it could build relationships in social media. But that's just the first part of the story. The truth is, there were many steps *after* creating that framework that were needed to reach implementation of the Zoetis EQStable page. These include channel selection, content creation, topic mix selection, promotion, and more. In this chapter I'll walk through the tactical side of great content programming.

Channel Selection

A big part of party planning is deciding where to throw the shindig, right? Channel selection is incredibly important to the success of any social implementation. More and more brands are wanting to go cross–social channel, and with that comes the challenges of quality and scale. Stretching yourself too far is a great way to set yourself up for failure.

When brands are new on social, they tend to get excited and want to be everywhere. But can you afford it? Do you have the team you need to deploy it? For most, it makes sense to onboard yourself in stages. Better to go deep first, and develop good usage patterns and some success stories before spreading across too many channels. Pick the channel that is the best match for your party and fits with your objectives, goals, and target audience.

Speaking generally, most brands end up on Facebook first because it's the biggest social game in town, still representing 65 percent of the playing field. The next biggest audience is Twitter, which is about 20 percent. Everything else combined makes up the remaining 15 percent.

Looking back at Zoetis, we considered but quickly discarded the idea of a private community site. Facebook adoption would be much easier, since we could expect most of the audience to be there already. There wasn't a need for privacy, and membership cachet wasn't likely to be the initial selling point.

Facebook was also a strong medium for the kind of community and content sharing the brand was hoping to inspire: stories and images about owning and caring for horses. We would complement the program with Pinterest and YouTube, but Facebook made sense as the primary hub.

A Buffet of Content Models

Your participation in social can't consist of throwing content onto a wall in bits and pieces over time. To be effective, it needs a purpose that adds up to something that serves customers more than it promotes the brand. What content model is the right fit for your customer and brand? The models that follow aren't mutually exclusive, and they don't claim to encompass all social media, but they help provide a focal point as you consider the range of types of interactions and experiences your customers might be looking for.

Social content models can be hybrids—EQStable, for example, is a combination of a "how-to community" and a "topical community"—and you might invent your own. Think through what kind of model you are pursuing, then develop content programming plans (with a focus on conversation) and deploy them—keeping in mind that it's all organic and will change as you go. But having a content model gives you a context in which to manage your adaptations and tie them back to the program's original goals.

You might think of these examples as being on a spectrum of benefits that ranges from practical to emotional. Sometimes social media deployments start out using practical models, then transition into more social-emotional ones. But anywhere along the spectrum, the very best are built around dialogue and relationships that together express a unique social brand identity.

Customer-to-customer (C2C) support communities: These are usually searchable, forum-based community sites or pages where customers support each other. C2C support empowers customers by acknowledging that they collectively know the product better than the company does, and creates a more responsive, comprehensive support structure than the company could manage alone—while also reducing costs. Generally the content is question driven ("How do I...?" or "What is...?") and includes a rating system to allow users to elevate the best answers. C2C support communities also help companies identify areas where products or communications can be improved, as in Apple's customer support forums. Finally, they build a library of customer-driven content, a value in itself, and a search engine optimization (SEO) driver.

What makes C2C support communities so successful is that they serve all those primal needs I've discussed: self-expression when users create content; making friends when they give help to and receive help from others; recognition because the folks that help others the most rise in status in the community. And then there is the benefit of getting one's problem actually solved. That's important too, but not as long lasting as the social benefits involved.

How-to communities: These are enthusiast communities where users exchange tips, hacks, and how-tos for "smart use" of the product. You see these frequently in the computer and video game industry, for example the Nintendo forums. But the same model works well in the cosmetics and beauty category, as you can see on Neutrogena's Facebook page, where the brand asks questions like, "What's your go-to makeup for going from a big presentation to a big night out?" and fans share ideas. Again, this kind of community hits all three primal needs and gives customers practical info on getting the most out of the brand's product. The brand benefits as well: The more ideas people have for using the product, and the more they hear about it, the more likely they are to purchase it. And of course, seeing first-hand who's using the product and how offers considerable market learning and an inherent customer-to-customer endorsement.

Networking communities: These communities create business value by fostering new professional relationships, connecting people to opportunities they might not have otherwise discovered, and creating a fluid environment for sharing knowledge (the B2B version of tips, hacks, and how-tos). The American Express Open Forum for entrepreneurs and small businesses is one such community. It's benefitted users by addressing issues they discuss. For example, American Express noticed a lot of entrepreneurs chatting about the difficult issue of getting paid on time. This led to new site content targeting that persistent problem, as well as a TV commercial on the subject. As an entrepreneur myself,

I can tell you that when I first heard the commercial—with phrases like "I could use help in getting my business paid on time"—my ears perked up and I thought, "Here's a brand that's made for *me*."

Event series: These are promoted events that could be entertainment or education oriented. A brand might sponsor a "Twitter chat," as *People* magazine has done with guests such as celebrity trainer Harley Pasternak. Other examples include Google Hangouts or webinars with a company representative or a celebrity in advance of a product launch. Events might promote the sale of specific products, drive customer acquisition, or encourage future engagement. They can be integrated with offline events like trade shows or award shows.

Volume often isn't the best measure of success for social media events. As with a mall event or trade show seminar, the role they play is one of content marketing, a reference vehicle for the greater promotion surrounding them. If you run ads about the event that reach your target impressions goal, you've succeeded even if only a limited number of people actually come to the event. Also factor in that usually 5 to 10 as many people hit the transcript or recorded video of the event as catch the event live—that is, *if* you have a good plan in place to transcribe it, then quickly get it edited, posted, and promoted. And now you will! Events create high-profile content that's useful as a basis for building awareness or driving customers to pages, sites, stores, or promotional action. They're terrific for customer name acquisition, and after the event, the content can be added to a library to attract customer interest and help with SEO.

Expert opinion networks: Useful (and sometimes vociferous) opinions are the currency-in-trade of these sites, but they also satisfy a participant's emotional need to be heard and recognized as an expert. Armchair expertise commonly drives blog circles, news and media websites, and product and service review sites. Generally these sites create status and recognition for top contributors based on both posting volume and quality, as rated by fellow users. We worked for many years on the *TV Guide* community site, where the magazine's top writers blogged. Community members appreciated the direct access and became bloggers and critics themselves. The site, like other expert opinion networks, built a deep content library and added to customers' enjoyment of the regular publication and their favorite TV shows. And as with any successful community site, word-of-mouth marketing gave the brand a big boost.

Topical communities: These focus on subject matter that links interested target customers together. For example, horses in the Zoetis EQStable, or cars in the MINI Cooper Owner's Lounge. Usually the brand brings substantial content assets to this model, and creates a space and culture for customers to do the same. Often the topic is directly linked to the product, but not always. For example, a shipping company might research its customers and find that in shipping departments they are all wearing headphones and listening to music. Music links these folks together, and the brand could use that connection as the seed for social community, demonstrating that the brand understands them better than its competitors do.

Cause communities: Here the conversation and content are focused on activism or interest in a philanthropic cause, usually somehow linked to the business' brand. Examples include the Dove Campaign for Real Beauty, which has the goal of increasing women's self-esteem by combatting unrealistic social expectations around female beauty, and the American Express Members Project, a community site focused on social impact. In the latter, members submitted, discussed, and voted on ideas for charitable causes. A panel of scholars picked a winner, and the company gave more than $1 million to an established charitable organization to implement the idea.

Often a cause-focused social venue provides extremely important emotional support to the people who are affected by the issue at hand, and to their families and the people working on the issue. The community and the attention the cause receives let them know they're not alone. On top of that, cause communities and campaigns done right truly help effect positive social change by building awareness, recruiting volunteers, or raising funds. Many studies and surveys have shown that customers are more loyal to brands they perceive as socially responsible and aligned with issues they care about. There's also a less-remarked-about but significant benefit from getting behind a cause: your employees will think more of your brand and be proud to work at a company that cares about something beyond the bottom line. The nonprofit Net Impact's *Talent Report: What Workers Want in 2012* is one of several studies that have shown that the majority of millennials now entering the workforce want a job that creates positive social impact, and are even willing to take a pay cut for it. Those who have such jobs report higher satisfaction compared to those who don't. I've seen that the effect is enhanced when you let the employees be active participants in the community or campaign, which in turn further personalizes and socializes your brand.

Show-character communities: These are fan communities and social tools driven by viewers' passion for or identification with shows and their favorite characters. Sometimes they allow users to "brand" themselves with particular show graphics or character personas, within the community or throughout their social presence. Users can also meet and discuss the shows with fellow die-hard fans. AMC's "Mad Men Yourself" tool even allows you to create your own character avatar and broadcast it wherever you have a social media presence. When LiveWorld worked with a premium cable channel to create and manage its online community website, the channel had huge success allowing users to dress their profiles in the graphics of favorite shows. Writers can listen to these communities, see how the audience is responding to a show's themes, and use that as inspiration to further develop the stories. Last but not least, the social programming itself can become a revenue center, with advertisers eager to be present where the fans are most active.

Social societies: Initially organized around practical or topical conversations, a social society develops into a full-blown sense of place that people effectively live in. This means they spend considerable time there, as a center point in their business and/or personal lives. Members form trusting community bonds, and every aspect of their lives becomes a potential subject of conversation and discussion. Sometimes when the members bond and talk about so many aspects of their lives, brands become frustrated and wish members were talking more about their product. But such societies attain the ultimate social media goal—an emotional connection in which the brand becomes a daily part of users' identity, and the community becomes a virtual third space that's as important as their real-world home. eBay, which I've mentioned before, is a classic example. What started as a sellers' support community evolved into a full-blown society, covering every aspect of the sellers' business needs and their personal lives as well: kids, travel, hobbies, aspirations, entertainment, health, etc.

You can see another example of a social society on the members-only user forums for Weight Watchers, where groups organize around weight loss goals, but over time members find themselves discussing major life events, such as weddings and promotions, as often as they do the pounds they've shed. As in other social societies, relationships in the forums oftentimes become offline relationships as well. One of my own colleagues has been friends for six years with several people she met on the Weight Watchers forums, and they've helped each other stay on the diet more than once.

Follow the Lead of the Customer

Your social media programming needs to cater to the online interests and behaviors of your target audience, and then successfully engage them around those interests. A particular campaign might seem like the perfect fit for your goals and objectives, but if it's not the perfect fit for your audience, it's not going far.

As you consider targets, make a smart evaluation of the assets and opportunities that exist to support a campaign, and look for easy wins. A few years back, we had a retail discount store client that saw a great organic opportunity to leverage: customers were independently showing off their best bargains from the stores in social media. Being a brick-and-mortar retailer, the brand was also interested in a campaign that would directly drive in-store traffic. So we developed a program for this client with two central features. First, we built an online community with profiles that allowed people to upload photos of their deals with a scroll-over that revealed the incredible bargain price. This let people re-experience that moment of victory—the brand's core selling proposition—when they flipped the tag, and then share it with fellow treasure hunters.

Second, since the brand was also looking to do something directly connected to in-store traffic, we created a way for shoppers on the floor to upload codes with their mobile phones that would alert other members on the community site to great bargains on goods that they had self-reported interest in. We put a lot of effort into this second piece. It seemed like such a clever way to bring people into the stores. But since mobile technology at the time was still pretty limited, the execution was no walk in the park.

The shared-deal experience feature of the site took off right away—customers loved it, because it allowed them to do what they were already doing themselves with a fun and improved feature set. But the mobile program? It never really got off the ground. Not enough customers were ready to use their cell phones as anything but phones, and many stores neglected to put up the signs that made the whole program work. You could say we were ahead of the times. And because we loved the idea so much, we held on to it longer than we probably should have.

As you implement a social media strategy, shoot for planned flexibility without losing sight of business objectives. Those objectives are the anchor that keeps execution from running amok. Pay close attention as you get to know your followers in the social space, and, even more important, as they get to know each other. You never know what unexpected obstacles, assets, and opportunities will emerge.

The real fun of the game in social—and where the biggest wins derive—is in being nimble enough to follow your customers' lead.

Getting People to the Party

As a rule, launching a social platform takes up-front promotion and then lots of work to keep that audience's attention. There's tons of competition and algorithms, at least on Facebook, that quickly block your posts from reaching fans if you're not actively engaging them.

The good news is that advertising your social efforts on Twitter and Facebook is both effective and inexpensive. Best are the ads with creative specifically designed for the social channel they're appearing in. For Facebook, ads are shareable content that appear in fans' newsfeeds or are otherwise presented as "sponsored stories." For Twitter, ads appear as "promoted tweets." The trend is toward text, photos, and stories that have a narrative and can be shared and discussed, offering a social experience. Traditional ads that simply repeat slogans, tout the product, or rely on flashy agency creative are generally poorly received.

Zoetis offers a good example of a successful ad-supported launch. To launch EQStable, the team drove early membership through paid advertising and promotion, which included Facebook advertising targeting "female," "US," and "horses," with a strong call to action and value proposition; banners and promoted content; joint promotion with another marketing initiative; the EQStable App; paid promotion; cross-venues; and weekly and one-time contests.

Zoetis also used partner marketing and leveraged ongoing relationships with organizations such as the American Quarter Horse Association, the Cowboy College, and the Future Farmers of America for content sharing and referral traffic. And finally, the brand made a concerted effort to feature the new page across its marketing mix, the single most important form of promotion to create sustainable traffic.

Best Practices for Great Party Conversation—a.k.a. Social Content Programming

What follows are some tried and true best practices for creating social media content. They are guidelines, not hard rules. Your audience ultimately sets the rules. The goal is to stimulate dialogue and engagement, and it's up to you to bring a flexible, curious mindset to the game.

I. Shoot for a 20/40/40 topic mix.

Most companies are so anxious to push out product messaging that they crowd out the conversation that keeps the party engaging. That's the legacy of decades of one-way mass marketing. And besides, the best companies love their products and services and, with that, love talking about them. But in social that's not what gets you engagement, loyalty, word of mouth, and long-term sales growth. Going back to the party metaphor, what gets you noticed in social is lots of interesting conversation, mostly not about you, but about your guests. This is even more the case on Facebook due to its pro-social algorithm, which manages which of your posts show up in a fan's newsfeed. It's a complicated bit of black magic, but here's the simple version: the more social your content is, the more people interact with it, the more Facebook will deliver it to people in their newsfeeds.

Thanks to the algorithms and the fundamental social behavior of people, it breaks down like this: if 80 percent of your posts are brand and product oriented, fewer people will see posts about your brand than if you had only had 20 percent brand product posts, and filled the other 80 percent with category and social posts, on topics of daily interest in your customers' lives. So if you want more people to see messages about your brand, post those messages less often. It may be counterintuitive, but it's true.

Making things even more challenging, Facebook continues to tweak its algorithm. Changes in late 2013 and early 2014 have led to many brands watching in dismay as their organic reach plummets. It's important for social marketers to stay up to date as Facebook and other channels constantly evolve. But it's safe to say that the trend is toward social content that provides value for users and stimulates conversation, not constant brand-centric promotion.

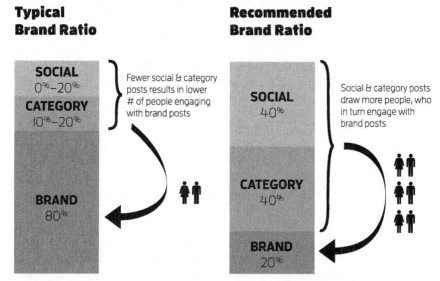

Typical Brand Ratio

SOCIAL 0%–20%
CATEGORY 10%–20%
BRAND 80%

Fewer social & category posts results in lower # of people engaging with brand posts

Recommended Brand Ratio

SOCIAL 40%
CATEGORY 40%
BRAND 20%

Social & category posts draw more people, who in turn engage with brand posts

Here's an example. As summer approaches, a retailer has the business goal of taking advantage of the season and selling a lot of barbecues. In traditional marketing, the retailer pushes out messages that tout the barbecue and the special seasonal price. In social marketing, the messaging is going to look like this:

20% brand: Acme BBQ with great features, $99 at our store!
40% category: Which do you like more, gas or charcoal BBQs?
40% social: Your favorite part of a July 4th BBQ is _____?

This weighted topic mix is a good rule of thumb for social. Of course, there are exceptions, but your fans' behavior and the performance of various posts will quickly tell you if you're one of them. Don't be fooled by high response (Likes or even sales) to a product post. First, such posts tend to generate impulse behaviors, not sustained revenue growth, where much greater value lies. Second, a product post can always be improved by being more social or being in the context of a series of social posts.

The success of product posts can also vary by program or channel context. On Twitter, for example, we've noticed that many brands are able to tweet with much higher frequency about the product without losing followers. It could be that many people connect to a brand on Twitter specifically *because* they're interested in a stream of news that's specifically about the brand or the product. And Facebook is more social in nature, some brands have such a strong following based on their products that enthusiasts want to spend time discussing them in detail with fellow fans. So start with 20 (brand)/40 (category)/40 (social) and develop your topic mix as you measure engagement over time.

2. Content and length should be tailored to the channel.

As soon as you're pushing out the same exact post through multiple social channels, you're not listening to customers or responding attentively. You're just broadcasting. This often is what brands do in an attempt to scale, and in doing so they make a double-whammy mistake. First of all, different channels are geared toward different kinds of content, so your messaging will sound tone deaf when automated across channels. Second, many times audiences are active in more than one channel. Those users get hit with identical messages from you, and they view it as spam—generally *not* known as one of the better ways to improve customer relationships.

Finally, if you're automating posts across channels, it's unlikely your community managers are really hearing, understanding, and relating to customers in those venues. That's a worst-practice route. Social media is intended to reduce the qualitative distance between your customers and your people, not push them further apart.

Twitter allows for 140 characters, but stick to 100 as a best practice so that people can retweet multiple times without having to edit posts for length. Twitter is an ideal medium to deliver informational, topical tidbits that are interesting enough that people will share them. It's also a good medium to tease longer-form content hosted on a blog, company site, or Facebook page.

On Facebook, status updates can exceed 140 characters, but as in social generally, short and pithy wins every time. Human social behavior as well as Facebook's algorithms give more weight to images, and such posts naturally get more attention. Posts designed to stimulate conversation are more appropriate here than on Twitter, thanks to the social focus of Facebook and to a platform structure that's more supportive of continuing conversations over time.

3. Don't over focus on posting frequency to create the feeling of responsiveness.

Contrary to popular belief, engagement in social media isn't always about being there 24/7—that's great, but not always needed, although companies offering customer service support in social may find themselves moving in that direction. To create the feeling that you're responsive, it's much more important to tailor your content programming and engagement to the context you're in, rather than trying to be everywhere all the time. That means paying attention to your channel, timing, and the dynamics of your target audience.

For most companies, posting frequency is somewhere between three times a day and three times a week—a broad range. If you don't have the resources to engage in conversation three times a week, you're not ready to step into social. Meanwhile, if you post too frequently, you'll crowd out your customers from engaging with each other. These are starting guidelines. We have clients who post more than three times a day with great success. But remember, how often you post is not the same as how often you are present and responding. The more you are present, the better. We encourage brands to respond to between 10 and 40 percent of posts and comments.

Real-time engagement is much more important to being social on Twitter than it is on Facebook. Many companies use Twitter successfully as a broadcasting tool—but to really engage in conversation there, you have to react quickly. For Twitter, a best practice is round-the-clock coverage, because you generally have to jump into a hot conversation in real time to participate. Facebook is different, since the application shuffles posts back into users' newsfeeds as conversation continues. Also, customers tend to browse full pages rather than looking at just the latest comments, allowing for more asynchronous conversation.

4. Use clear calls to action to boost engagement.

If you want to engage people, make it easy: tell them. Include implicit calls to action in posts by asking a question, offering a fill-in-the-blank, or requesting that they share a story or photo. (Asking for Likes will get you more Likes, but that in itself doesn't create true and sustainable engagement. In fact, Facebook considers such posts spam and penalizes your content through the algorithm.)

5. Establish a posting cadence.

It's no accident that magazines and newspapers have content templates that they replicate in every issue. The repetition allows readers to feel at home in the publication, with favorite bits that they turn to first every time. The same is useful in social media. Create regular content features that your customers can expect and look forward to—it'll help them get ready to contribute themselves. Throwback Thursday and Follow Friday are probably the most generic, widespread examples, but be creative and find formats that fit your content and cultural model.

6. Think visuals, visuals, visuals.

Photographs outperform text alone every time. Microvideo is also on the rise, so look at that too, though its popularity is currently dwarfed by that of photos, and likely to remain so.

7. There's no real rule of thumb for posting frequency.

Do you have something truly useful, fun, witty, or relevant to say, and an audience that wants to hear it? Let that be your guide. You can benchmark off your competitors and industry metrics, but at the end of the day, your own social metrics and qualitative customer feedback are your best guide. Again and again, our clients ask for formulas or silver bullets to become successful in social media, like how to calculate the perfect time to post. These can be helpful, but the impact is marginal compared to that of getting the topic mix and conversational tone right, so that you can engage in organic, real-time dialogue. After all, we are doing real-time marketing here.

8. Abandon corporate jargon or legalspeak.

It really has no place in social. If there comes a time when it's needed, direct folks to a static page rather than using legalese in a social conversation. More on that coming soon in chapter 8, Turning the Social Minefield into Opportunity.

I want to close this chapter with the most important best practice of all: **put people first.** Howard Schultz titled his first book, about the birth and growth of Starbucks, *Pour Your Heart into Every Cup*. As you build your company's social media success, remember that. Your team needs to pour its heart—whatever that means for *your* brand—into every post and every conversation.

Social in Action: Become the Starbucks of Social Media

I first got to know Starbucks CEO Howard Schultz in the late '90s, when we produced a virtual live event featuring him and Mark McGuire speaking on behalf of a social cause. The event took place on Talk City, the consumer community website LiveWorld created and managed during that period.

During the run-throughs before the live event, Schultz immediately felt that something special was going on with this social media form—so much so that he arranged a call with me, the CEO of this Internet start-up.

"Hello, I'm Howard Schultz, the CEO of a food service chain called Starbucks," he said when we got on the phone. "You may have heard of it." He seemed, and would later prove to be, very genuine and unassuming.

"Let me see ... Do I know it?" I answered. "Hmmm. Is that the one that sells coffee on every single street corner?"

That broke the ice, and we've been friends ever since. Howard was taken by the way that Talk City created an environment for personable social connection in a virtual space. He immediately recognized that it was the same thing he was doing with Starbucks' physical spaces, where his vision was to create a third space beyond home and work, where people could experience a social environment and connect with others. Howard told me that LiveWorld was, in fact, the Starbucks of the Internet, and as such it was something he wanted to be a part of. Starbucks soon became an investor.

Just as in Talk City's chats and forums, and in well-managed social media spaces today, Starbucks uses technology, process flow, and culture to create a consistent, high-quality experience for customers. The baristas are considered the key to the entire model, just as moderators and community managers are key in social media. Starbucks calls its baristas *partners* rather than *employees* to mark the centrality of their role.

What Howard understands, and what anyone marketing a brand in social media needs to understand, is this: your brand's social space will be most successful as a *people* experience, not a product experience. Starbucks stores are successful because they create an emotional connection among customers, which in turn enables the brand to create an emotional connection with them—reliably and at scale.

Social media offers the same potential for your brand, so long as you, the CMO, see it as a place to make real human connections, rather than just broadcasting brand content at people and running the thing off algorithms and canned responses. The environment you're designing in social may have many functions, but it must put people, dialogue, and relationships first.

Chapter 6 Key Takeaways:

✓ If you're resource constrained—and by resources I mean time to develop content and conversation, not just the size of your ad budget—go deep in one channel rather than spreading yourself too thin across multiple channels.

✓ To ensure that your content serves customers more than it promotes the brand, don't just throw posts at the wall and see what sticks. Work with a conversational content model in mind that communicates purpose and value to customers.

✓ A particular campaign might seem the perfect fit for your goals and objectives, but if it's not the perfect fit for your audience, it's not going to work.

✓ Social spaces don't launch themselves; any new social effort needs advertising and marketing to get off the ground.

✓ Great social content puts the customer first, creating value through dialogue and relationships. Limit brand-focused, promotional posts to 20 percent of your content.

Chapter 7:
Master the Art of Social Storytelling

Harness the power of social storytelling to get more attention, more engagement, and deeper customer relationships.

"Stories rise above individual products," said Olivier François, the CMO of Chrysler, at the October 2013 annual meeting of the Association of National Advertisers. By transcending business as usual, storytelling provides an opportunity for you to connect with your customers, and for your customers to connect to each other. Stories engage people's emotions and are a powerful conduit to communicate values and contextual meaning, opening the door to deeper customer commitment.

The use of stories to entertain, influence, educate, and connect is very old. Humankind used storytelling to communicate ideas and values long before the birth of written language. They shared stories orally, painted them on rock walls, carved them into trees, even tattooed or sliced them into their bodies. Storytelling has always been social, too, with individual tellers embellishing, adding details, altering key plot points, and tailoring characters and images to ignite the interest of their particular audiences.

Today we understand more about why stories are so potently persuasive, thanks to several decades of sociological and psychological research mining the connection between emotional response and learning. As the movie producer and business mogul Peter Guber writes in *Tell to Win,* "Stories that work transport people emotionally." It turns out that if your story is good enough to rev up people's emotions, your audience is much more likely to internalize and remember the information and values you seek to communicate. Providing them with a list of data points and abstract statements making your case doesn't stick like a story will.

One-Way Storytelling in Marketing and Advertising

Traditional advertisers have gotten better and better at exploiting the power of story. Big-budget commercials set up clever scenarios, offer compelling challenges, and then provide resolution—the product! These days, you can also see the customer-centric effect of social media on traditional ads: Even brand-produced ads increasingly attempt to allow customers to experience stories from their own POV. Brands know that those are the ads that get shared and commented on.

In 2012, 8 million people watched as skydiver Felix Baumgartner, sponsored by Red Bull, plummeted from the stratosphere, via a camera that allowed them to experience the fall live, and from his POV. That same year, Nike created an ad campaign called Just Do It: Possibilities that showed average Joes doing incredible things in their Nikes: a runner outracing a movie star, a kid scoring a goal in professional soccer, a cyclist riding a mechanical bull.

Ten years ago, celebrity endorsements would say, "Drink/use/buy this product because I do!" Now celebrities stand in for the common person. The ads that feature them seem to say, *"I'm like you,* and that's why we're both using this product." As an example, take a look at the Nike video "Training Day," which follows NBA star LeBron James off-season as he joins hundreds of Miami residents on a cross-town bike ride.

But increasingly, customers want even more, especially when it comes to advertising that they interact with as part of their social experience. Slickness and high production values are of less interest than authenticity and stories about real, relatable people, especially if the story is actively shaped by the customers. Think of the huge success of reality TV versus scripted series. People like to keep it real—produced, but real.

Certainly, great storytelling is happening in brand-produced advertising, but its impact is limited by its one-way nature. Context—the medium—matters. Take an example from the early days of Internet advertising in the late '90s. The vast majority of web advertising took place in the form of banner ads on the first wave of search engines—Yahoo, Infoseek, Lycos, and Excite. Banner ads made sense on those sites, because users came to search engines intending to have an experience that would quickly take them to another site. In that context, banner ads successfully encouraged click-throughs.

The Trouble with Broadcasting in a Social World

Fast-forward a few years, as banners proliferated across other kinds of sites. Very quickly, people began ignoring the banners and stopped clicking. They were happily consuming the content they had gone to the site to experience, and had little to no interest in clicking away to advertising. If they did, they left quickly to get back to the site that held their interest.

At the time, we worked with a top consumer packaged goods brand whose marketing leaders were among the first to realize that context mattered on the web; a new ad format was needed if customers were to pay attention. That brand began to create story-based ads that popped up when a banner was clicked. This approach enabled the team to tell a better story than they could in a banner ad, but without forcing customers to go to a new site. I know how successful those ads were, because that brand was the biggest advertiser on LiveWorld's consumer community site Talk City; they wanted more ad inventory than we had to offer. They created the pop-up story ad because they knew that the best marketing is storytelling, and that their ads needed to fit the context of the environment they were in. In the case of Talk City, it was an early social media experience where customers were heavily engaged in discussions with each other, but had conversation gaps where they would happily look at an engaging story ad, as long as it didn't take them away from their social activity.

And today, as a marketer, you're competing for their hearts and minds in the context of their newsfeeds, where they're getting the information that they care most about—friends' messages and topics they've chosen to follow. You can't interrupt something people care about with something they care about less (your snappy-but-one-way, brand-centric, produced story). To get and keep their attention, you need to tell a story that they care about as much as the stories they're telling and hearing from their friends, the stories that affect and lend meaning to their everyday lives.

The easiest way to make sure your content matters to them is to enlist them in making it. If they're helping you tell the story, it becomes part of their identity, the core of what adds import and value to their lives.

In Social Storytelling, the Customer Co-Creates

If you want to put your finger on the zeitgeist of brand storytelling today, watch the 2013 GoPro ad "Lions—the New Endangered Species?" Actually, you could watch any GoPro ad, but I like this one because the lions are cuddly. Over 32 million people have watched it, wanting to see what life and lions look like from the point of view of "lion whisperer" Kevin Richardson. If you're not familiar with GoPro, it's the camera gadget that clips on to helmets or just about anything else and lets viewers experience incredibly interesting POVs—from a bicycle, a surfboard, or inside the embrace of a lion. They've been used to film all of Red Bull's extreme sports videos and, most famously, Baumgartner's space jump.

The genius of GoPro's content marketing—and why the company's videos are immensely viral—is that they don't feel like ads. The vast majority of them are made by customers, and the ones produced in-house are terrifically visual, quality narrative storytelling.

I'd argue that the popularity of the videos and of the technology itself is due to something even more specific. GoPro is a zeitgeist product, the perfect technology for the kinds of stories (marketing and otherwise) that customers are finding increasingly desirable in the highly interactive, social media–enhanced world. The company has seen its growth double since its founding.

Today, customers want stories that put them in the driver's seat, either as characters, narrators, or authors. And in social, the most successful stories are those in which customers themselves are creative agents, which is why GoPro's customer-submitted content performs so well.

The most successful brands are finding ways to tell stories that increase customer agency and tap into the customer's *emotional* perspective—not just by satisfying aspirational fantasies, but by meeting customers where they are: by making their lives the fuel for narrative, both fictional and nonfictional.

You don't have to be GoPro to embrace this in your marketing. Include actual customer stories as part of your evolving brand story. The stories should convey brand attributes in a memorable context, to entertain and educate customers and keep them interested. If you do this well, you'll inspire customers to spread the word about you, creating lifelong fans and advocates.

True social storytelling, in which customers themselves drive the stories that define brands, isn't that common yet. There are plenty of tactical best practices for collaborative storytelling in an asynchronous, interactive medium. But most companies are still focused on broadcasting content created by their marketing team, pushing it out through social channels, and then hoping for applause in the form of Likes and comments. But however entertaining it tries to be, most brand content is still the annoyance that interrupts the content we want—whether it's a favorite TV show or our friends' photos.

How Does Social Storytelling Work?

Social storytelling is collaborative, engaging the audience in the creation and development of the story as it unfolds and changes in real time. The customer becomes a character in the story, the narrator, or even the writer.

In 2013, Honda used customer-led social storytelling to drive an entire campaign. The brand asked customers who had driven their cars over 100,000 miles to submit their stories. Then the brand created a Honda Stories YouTube channel. Later, it aired television commercials during Sunday football featuring poignant snapshots of actual Honda drivers experiencing life's peak moments—a wedding, prom, a weekend trip—with their cars.

Honda didn't just tell a story that it thought customers would like. It asked *the customer* to tell the story, and thereby share the job of defining the brand experience, and even its values. Rather than create a story, it created guidelines and a framework that made it easier for customers to come forward and connect via their greatest car-related experiences. In social storytelling, truth is often greater than any fiction the brand could develop, no matter how good its creative team.

A panel at the 2014 South by Southwest Interactive conference in Austin asked, "Has social killed storytelling?"—questioning whether the newsfeed has made our attention spans too short for stories. Of course social hasn't killed storytelling! Social has only raised the bar, forcing advertisers into a pattern of constant creativity and reinvention. The problem is often that, entrenched in the old way—crafting a story, packaging it up, and sending it out—most marketers have failed to reframe their role in the creative process. Today's brand storytellers shouldn't just be *creating* stories for social. Instead they should create the *framework* that facilitates the sharing and creation of stories by their customers; the framework that makes it safe and inspires customers to step up to the campfire.

Storytelling Frameworks to Involve Customers

Keep in mind that "storytelling" doesn't have to mean that you invent a fully imaginary character or world. You can tell stories and cast customers as characters in events that are happening in the real world, with your brand or in the broader cultural landscape. Just as you do when thinking about content, ask yourself: What do we have to work with? How does our brand naturally become a character in the everyday, real-life drama of our customers? Then, how can we engage our customers to tease those stories into conversation?

In true social storytelling, every customer is a potential character, with his or her own plot and theme in the story. The brand's social platform—and the brand or even the product itself—becomes a venue for customers to play, improvise, and create. The goal isn't just to engage them, but to emotionally *involve* them in a story where they play a lead role. That requires changing your perspective: The brand doesn't control the story. The brand gets the ball rolling by getting their attention and engaging them enough that they take ownership of the story.

Here are some suggested frameworks that make that possible—but your creativity is the only limit in developing others:

Launch a creation contest: Challenge your customers to tell a story in words or images about how your brand figures into their lives; set guidelines that help add structure to their task. A great example of a successful customer-creation contest was Lego's three-week Holiplay campaign in 2012. According to the agency, Konstellation, the aim of the campaign was "to create brand awareness and show an emotional connection between the Lego brand and key family moments during December." The approach wasn't just to *show* that connection, but to create a storytelling game that actively engaged families with Lego play during the holidays. Spreading the word through social, Lego asked fans to create five specific Lego characters, and then make their creations unique by photographing them in fun and surprising locations. People from 119 different countries participated, submitting videos that stunned Lego and fellow fans with their creativity. The best photographs became part of a short film that used the characters and images to tell a holiday fairy tale.

Social in Action: Rewarding Fans

Rewarding the customers who've actively engaged in your story is one of the best ways to increase engagement among the rest of your customers as well. That's why Old Spice didn't just ask fans to interact with its Old Spice Guy character, it turned to a superfan to release a major segment of the story in social.

Chris G., a high school kid from Missouri, had attracted the brand's attention by dressing as the Old Spice Guy for Halloween and doing his own re-enactment of the original ad spot on his YouTube channel, ShakeAndBakeGuy. The relationship kicked off with the Old Spice Guy calling Chris on the phone and videotaping the conversation, in which they talked about how Chris would have the exclusive on releasing the next commercial.

Chris put out a Twitter message telling people to follow him in order to be the first to get to see the new spot. He posted a screengrab from it and created a #NewOldSpiceAd hashtag to get buzz going. Finally he embedded the new ad on his personal and professional websites and—after a countdown on Twitter—released the link there with the message, "THE LATEST OLD SPICE COMMERCIAL IS NOW YOURS! ARE YOU MAN ENOUGH!?"

Create a character: In social storytelling today, you typically see a few different kinds of characters—customers, employees, even the product or brand itself can become a character. A well-known example of a character embodying a brand is the Old Spice Guy, "The Man Your Man Could Smell Like," according to the campaign's tagline. His story generated upwards of 1.8 billion impressions, as the CEO told *BusinessWeek*, and led to P&G reducing traditional ad spend in favor of social media. Five months after the campaign launched, *AdWeek* reported that "overall sales for Old Spice body-wash products are up 11 percent in the last 12 months; up 27 percent in the last six months; up 55 percent in the last three months; and in the last month, with two new TV spots and the online response videos, up a whopping 107 percent."

The brand created the Old Spice Guy character, but he came alive primarily through real-time dialogue with customers through Twitter and Facebook.

Involve customers in a brand story: What's going on with your brand that customers could become a part of? For example, in 2013 the MTV European Music Awards gave eight superfans the chance to announce the nominations in a particular award category. Also work on developing your core brand narrative, and use it to look for ideas around how to include customers in that ongoing story. Having a very clear story that embodies your values provides important continuity as stories and messaging are adapted for, or co-opted by, different groups.

Use prompts: As part of your day-to-day content, ask your followers questions that encourage storytelling. Fill-in-the-blank questions asking *who?* or *why?* are great story starters or check-ins to escalate the narrative or take it in another direction. Bold, declarative statements can also get a conversation started. For example, which do you think is likely to provoke a response and encourage someone to share a personal story?

1.   People are messy.

2.   Who's the messiest person in your house?

3.   Men are so MESSY!

The last statement, #3, is specific and extreme enough to create controversy among those who disagree with it, and sharing among those who are living with a messy, messy man.

Try reincorporation: Reincorporation is a trick used by actors in improvisational comedy, in which performers develop stories in real time with help from the audience. In improv, when the performers find a bit that gets a laugh, they bring it back a few more times during the rest of the performance, or find creative ways to reference it. They bring it back again and again, as long as people keep laughing.

Reincorporation helped the Old Spice Guy's story develop. The brand quickly realized that the videos got the biggest laughs when he was responding to what people said in social media—and once it realized that, it played the joke again and again. The brand never really changed the story format, it just kept reincorporating the audience response.

Plan content calendar arcs: As your brand builds a social presence centered on customer conversations, you are building content over time. In aggregate that content tells a story. It's likely to be a very disjointed story—*unless* you plan your content calendar and daily interactions with the principles of social storytelling in mind. Use themes to create a narrative arc for your messaging. To use a really simple example, for December's content, a brand might use the theme of "holiday chaos," following a customer as she plans and executes holiday events—encountering either disaster…or success!

Three Rules from Improv to Make Brand Stories More Engaging Than SNL

To master improvisational co-creation with customers, you'll need to develop two skills that can be really difficult for marketers: the agility to respond cleverly and creatively in real time, and the empathy to sense an audience's reaction and play off it. The better you understand the rules of improvisational theater, where stories are created in the moment and often rely heavily on feedback from the audience, the better you'll be at telling real-time stories in social. Mark Williams, LiveWorld's Creative Director of Social Strategy and Content Programming, has an MFA in theater, and that's no accident.

Here are some of Mark's best tips to help you understand the rules of improv so that the stories you tell in social are even funnier and more engaging than those you might find on a TV show (where the comedians play off each other but don't involve the audience), and infinitely more effective than the one-way stories offered in advertising.

Agree and say, "Yes, and…"

When improv players spontaneously develop a skit on stage, they eliminate "but" and "no" from their thought process. Instead, when another player adds an element to the conversation, they say, "Yes, and…," and then incorporate that new element as they move forward.

As you interact, listen to your followers and incorporate their feedback with the "Yes, and…" model, even (or maybe especially) if it departs from the story outcome you had in mind. Sometimes this could mean using a clever customer comment in your next communication. Other times you might look to analytics to tell you about the audience's preferences.

If you don't like what customers are saying, never delete comments or shut customers down. Instead, play with them and engage by saying yes. Of course, you can be selective and ignore some things, unless the noise becomes overwhelming.

Establish objectives and values, then give up control.

You know where *you* want the story to go, but the story that is being told may not be the story you wanted to tell. That's OK. You don't have to know how the story is going to end—it just needs to resonate with your brand's values and the objectives of your social campaign. Let the customers create, stepping in only when the story strays or needs an infusion of creative energy.

In short, go with the flow. Listen, say, "Yes, and...," and incorporate what is being said into the narrative. Then you will learn about influence, and most important, truly engage with your customers, even if the communication takes you to unexpected places. They will continue to engage with you as long as the story is compelling.

Fail big! Be bold in your ideas and execution.

There's nothing worse than a flat, boring prompt; customers tune out and maybe even remove you from their newsfeed. To create something truly memorable, be bold and shoot for a big win—even if it means the occasional big loss.

You'll generate more attention and engagement by failing big than by playing it safe. It will humanize you and endear you to some, and you can be sure that everyone will be paying attention. Though it may lose you a few fans, overall you'll have more attention for your next story. Also, many people are entertained by finding mistakes—embrace them. You just gave them an opportunity to show how smart they are!

There are no mistakes, only opportunities. The whole point of interacting with your customers is to entertain, inform, or inspire. We (both audience and brand) *learn* from mistakes. Just don't muck it up two or three times in a row. That's bad.

Chapter 7 Key Takeaways:

✓ Storytelling provides an opportunity for you to transcend your product and connect with your customers, and for your customers to connect with each other.

✓ The brand's job in social isn't to create and push the stories. It's to provide the framework and rewards that inspire customers to share their own stories.

✓ Authenticity is more important to engaging customers than slick production values.

✓ Context matters, and the stories that succeed best are those that customers see as being connected to their identity—and the quickest route to making that connection is getting them invested in the process of creation.

✓ Remember the rules of improvisational comedy. Say yes to new ideas, share control with customers, and be prepared to fail big rather than play it safe.

Chapter 8:

Turning the Social Minefield into Opportunity

Socialized brands don't just survive social media crises, they use them to build improved customer relationships.

"Never let a serious crisis go to waste...It's an opportunity to do things you could not do before." —Rahm Emanuel

Social media can make companies feel like they're walking a minefield—out of nowhere, from any direction, could come an explosion of deadly force. Really, that's no surprise. Social media can't be controlled by traditional PR models. Couple that with the fact that many companies hand their social media keys to part-time, sometimes inexperienced staff, or to outside agencies that don't have depth in the space. Then factor in the need for quick decision making and the intense pressure of knowing that a misstep could result in tens of thousands more irate comments; media reports (forever archived online), not just about the crisis but how you handled it; and real damage to customer perception and sales.

But as they say, in crisis lies opportunity: During a crisis, all attention is on your brand. If you embrace the moment to speak directly to customers, showing that the brand listens and cares, you can not just turn it around, but emerge with stronger relationships and a clearer brand identity than ever. Generally a crisis is caused by a real issue, but often paying proper attention to the people involved is more important in handling a crisis than the actual issue itself.

A social media crisis can take on many shapes, but broadly defined, it's a surge in social activity that disrupts the normal user experience to such an extent that it negatively affects either brand perception or the business goals of your company, requiring additional resources and rapid attention above normal workflow to manage. In 2013, the women's yoga-wear brand Lululemon had the worst kind of social media meltdown—the kind that has an impact on sales and stock value. The trouble started because customers were complaining that its most popular yoga pants had a serious problem: they were see-through. The situation got worse when founder and Chairman Chip Wilson defended the product line on Bloomberg TV by saying, "Quite frankly, some women's bodies just don't actually work." Earlier in the year, the company had already been criticized for favoring small sizes in store displays.

Backlash on social media was immediate, perhaps summed up best by @mel_catherine's November 7, 6:32 p.m. tweet, "I knew you couldn't trust $90 yoga pants."

As the negative comments stacked up, Lululemon did nothing. Finally, on day four, the company posted Wilson's apology video to YouTube. Many people judged it to be insincere. As of this writing, the video on YouTube has 60 Likes and 327 Dislikes, and Wilson has stepped down as the company's chairman. There has been even more crisis fallout; the CEO has also been replaced.

Lululemon made at least two of the six mistakes I see brands making in times of social crisis.

1. Waiting too long to respond

Usually a response is not delayed because no one on the team has noticed the issue. It's because they don't know how to respond or their hands are tied, and there's no clear chain of command to get answers and permission to act. And so while they all tear their hair out, the problem gets worse.

2. Getting defensive

Your customers perceive a problem, so there's a problem. Too many companies fight the feedback when they should be listening. Gather data, and let them know you take the matter seriously and are doing everything in your power to respond to them, even if you can't resolve the underlying issue.

3. Shoving problems under the rug

A perfect example is Applebee's 2013 debacle, when an employee was fired for posting the receipt of a customer who didn't tip. Company reps not only deleted negative comments about her firing from Facebook and elsewhere but also tried to hide their original (defensive) response. That made people all the more critical. The company went from being unfair in the eyes of the public to being unfair *and* deceptive.

Applebee's violated the number one rule of social: total transparency, total authenticity. Try to ignore, dismiss, delete, or control criticism, and customers will simply create their own forum. On the Internet another place to talk about you is always one click away—and so are millions of other customers instantly listening to the chatter, good or bad.

The Wrong Way to Handle Negative PR in Social Media

93

4. Forgetting to shut down or update the scheduled content calendar

When you're in the middle of a crisis and your scheduled status updates continue as planned, oblivious to the crisis, it seems like you're asleep at the wheel at best, and unsympathetic to the problem at worst.

5. Legalese

Legal counsel may need to be involved. But no one speaks legalese in the land of social media, or rather no one wants to listen to it. Responses there need to be in plain language that people understand.

6. Failing to participate in the conversation

Moderators need to be involved in the conversation, acknowledging concerns and making it clear that the company is listening. Moving the conversation to a separate site, with clear links, can be a good way to de-emphasize it or cover more detailed content—but don't try to shut down or ignore the criticism.

The Many Faces of Social Media Crisis

Social media crises come in many shapes and sizes. Here are some of the most common.

The Major Fail

Customers believe, accurately or not, that a product or service experience has failed to live up to the brand's promise. This belief could be based on a history of perceived failures or on a single, highly visible failure. Example: Lululemon's see-through yoga pants are explained by the CEO as the result of customers being too fat. #openmouthinsertfoot

The Rogue Employee

An employee makes a comment or shares content that puts the brand at risk. This could be an employee acting off the cuff in a way that doesn't represent the brand, or deliberate sabotage. Example: A video of a Pizza Hut employee urinating into one of the kitchen's sinks goes viral. #grossout

The "D'oh!"

A fracas results when a content item is misaligned with the audience either by error or oversight. The cause might be a simple misunderstanding of the audience, a good-natured but ill-received joke, or even a blatant posting error that publishes the wrong content in the wrong place at the wrong time. Example: Entenmann's uses the hashtag #notguilty in reference to eating tasty treats—not realizing the hashtag was trending thanks to the verdict in the high-profile Casey Anthony trial. #sloppy

The Spamalot

Users or bots post inappropriate content that offends customers. This is the most common issue seen on large-brand pages, and also the most easily managed with diligent monitoring and moderation. Example: Comment threads are full of links to Viagra distributors on a family-friendly site. #janitorneeded

The Activist

There is backlash or organized opposition from interest, identity, or political groups, including organized labor, environmental groups, etc. The opposition may be to a specific campaign, or it may be in protest of a particular product or perceived consequence of product usage. Activists may use social media to advocate and organize product boycotts and offline protests. Sometimes the complaints are legitimate, other times they may manufacture or distort issues as a means of attacking the brand. Example: A fraudulent, viral photo of an allegedly many-years-old but undegraded McDonald's cheeseburger won't quit making the rounds. #debunked

It's Easier to Catch a Tadpole Than a Frog: Creating a Crisis Plan

The key to social media crisis management is in providing guidelines to *everyone* in your company that make it crystal clear exactly what they should do if they spot an issue. Otherwise minutes, often even hours, could be wasted in getting the problem to the right person's inbox. And in that time, a tadpole can become a frog—a story with legs that leaps not only off your brand page but across platforms and into traditional media headlines.

Most issues can be spotted by your social team, via social monitoring or your brand-owned page. But not infrequently, an employee from the broader organization will find a problem—which is why everyone in your company needs to know whom to direct issues to.

You and your team need to develop a crisis escalation policy that answers the following logistical questions:

✓ Is the threat low, medium, or high?

✓ For each crisis level, who should be notified?

✓ By what mechanism (email, phone, etc.)?

✓ Who will approve responses?

✓ How will updates be distributed to the responders?

✓ Who will monitor the situation and provide updates?

Assessing the Threat

It's important to calibrate the crisis level and then match your response to it. Too often companies jump to one extreme or the other, ignoring the crisis or overreacting, when most situations call for an in-between response. Everyone in your company, not just marketing, should have a simple crisis kit that designates levels of crisis and lets them know whom to contact for each level. It's simple and it's efficient. At LiveWorld, we customize these crisis levels according to a number of client variables, but the basic assessment we build from looks like this:

Risk Level	Description	Examples
Low	A series of complaints or issues that begins to look like a trend. OR A single brand mention or issue that has a story with significant gravity and outrage that may cause it to spread rapidly. OR A social crisis that is arising within the brand's industry or product space that has the potential to spread to your brand.	Complaints about an advertising campaign not being sensitive to a group A story of gross misbehavior by an employee or grievous injury from a product A competitor's involvement in a social crisis based on a product characteristic that your product shares
Medium	Repetitive posts on a single topic in a set time period and with a certain passion level. OR A concern that is gaining momentum and following on a single social channel or on multiple social channels.	Similar to low level, but with greater visibility and higher post levels
High	An explosive volume of comments on an individual subject or related topics with high passion levels. The content or audience is aggressively growing. There is usually a high-risk topic with high momentum and high spread, often to various channels (Facebook, Twitter, blogs, etc.).	Major company and product events or issues Issues that drive public outrage generally include a perception of injustice that is being viewed by a high-level audience

Your risk levels should be useful for both small-scale issues and large events.

Who's on First?

Once you've established those crisis levels, you need to decide who will be on the response teams. At every level (low, medium, and high), the team needs the authority to post a response. In other words, anyone whose input is required before a response can be made needs to be on the team.

Make sure you have a contact list for your crisis team that's adequately maintained; regularly updated, available to all team members, and ready to use when you least expect it, including after business hours and on weekends. (Check out the sample crisis contact list in the toolkit.)

Keep in mind that social crises are a sure way to attract the attention of the executive team. How you handle a crisis will either redouble or alleviate their suspicion that social is dangerous, unmanageable, and not to be trusted. So when it comes to your response teams, you want to make sure you have the best set of decision makers in the room. Likely candidates include:

- **Social media experts:** These team members will help research the situation and give color to the issue at hand to help in gauging the potential response. They will also help define the best method, tone, and location for a response.

- **PR and corporate communications teams:** PR teams have experience and often topic-specific knowledge that will assist in drafting the response. They're likely to need to approve any sensitive response. However, it's also important to adapt the approach to the dynamics of social media, which are different from traditional PR models.

- **Legal, regulatory, and corporate affairs teams:** These team members will aid in advising about what can and can't be said. Legal teams are not included to offer input on tone and voice. Let them know up front that fan/customer expectations, not legalese, need to determine the language of the response.

- **Subject matter experts:** If an issue is known or recurring (for example, if your company has been repeatedly targeted by a particular interest group), you ideally will have participants who intimately know the history of that issue, the causes, solutions, the depth of influence, etc. Guidance from these team members will ensure that you have the full scope of the issue before you respond to something you perceive as a one-off issue, but that may recur.

- **Business owner:** This is the team member that owns the area that hosts the social media site or is charged with social listening and response. This person has the final sign-off on any response to the event. The hierarchy level of this person will likely vary based on the severity of an event. Small and inconsequential events will likely have a middle manager in this role. Large events with high brand risk will likely require a higher-level decision maker.

Do Your Research

At the first sign of an issue, a designated member of your social team should immediately begin any research necessary to understand the context of the flagged issue. Identify the answers to these questions:

Who is the originator?

This can be hard to determine at times if the same information (urban legend–style) is being shared by many people. But if possible, finding the originator can help you understand his or her motivations. How you respond depends on whether the originator is a customer, a market influencer, an employee, a competitor, or an activist.

What is the originator's motivation?

Is the originator looking for help or just venting to the world? Is he or she passionate about a cause? If you're dealing with someone who genuinely needs help, interaction will often help right away. But if you're dealing with a frequent brand critic or organized political attack, then a response often just incites the originator further. There are people who spend their lives creating chaos for brands, and often research identifies if you're dealing with a so-called troll.

What is the substance behind the issue and the company's position on it?

You don't want to be flying blind when dealing with a crisis. Find out what's going on as best you can. Get clear on your company's position on the matter. It may be different from what people think or want it to be. Whatever it is, you will have to be transparent and authentic (but not defensive or argumentative) about it.

Is this a known adversary?

Is this a customer whose comments have escalated 25 times already, or is this a first timer? Is this person part of an organized group that is targeting the brand?

Is there a history related to this person's issue?

If you search broadly on the web, do you find mentions of similar product issues? If so, this creates a rallying point for others to join the conversation and escalates the frustration of the poster.

What is the originator's relationship to the brand/company?

If this is a former employee who has a lawsuit pending against the company, you need to know that. If this is an employee of a competitor, that is also important to know. Research his or her background.

Evaluate the Actual Risk to the Brand

Now that you have a better picture of the story behind the post, step back and look at the potential risk of the situation. Here you're essentially making a much more nuanced version of the threat assessment, which will inform your response. To evaluate the risk, consider:

What is the influence level of the people discussing the topic?

If someone has a new social media account with only five followers, you can make the situation worse by responding and introducing all of your followers to the story. If one of the participants has a huge following, on the other hand, a response may be needed.

Is the conversation volume growing or declining?

Most social media crisis events have a relatively short life cycle. Be sure you have a feel for where in this cycle you are. If the cycle is slowing, commenting may just breathe life back into it. Pause to review thoroughly before reacting.

What outreach options do you have?

Depending on the social channel, you may have limited opportunities to reach out directly or privately to the original commenter. Consider all your options.

What is the potential for public outrage?

A single person with a mundane product complaint doesn't attract much attention. A single indignant person with an unusual story gets plenty. Example headlines we have dealt with: "My wife was attacked outside of <business name> and they didn't care." "How <business name> put my son's life at risk." "How <product name> caused (injury/illness/death)." Items that strike an emotional chord or suggest a threat to other customers have a much higher likelihood of going viral. And if there are pictures to accompany such a story, you're at code red.

Is the topic high risk?

Is this a topic your team has already identified as high risk? Do the issue or the responses have legal ramifications? If so, the potential for many more uninvolved parties to join the bandwagon is high.

To Respond or Not to Respond

With the above research, your team should have enough information to make an educated decision about whether to respond or not. Sometimes, even in what appears to be a high-level crisis, standing down—or at least pausing before responding—is the right answer.

As you consider whether to respond, consider these factors:

- **Is it required by regulations?** In some industries, government regulations require companies to respond and gather contact information in some social situations—for example, if someone were to comment that a medication made him or her nauseated.

- **Will a response reset the conversation?** Usually we see these opportunities when there is gross misinformation, or an actual customer with a problem that can be solved. If your response is to defend the brand, don't. People don't believe brands in these situations, and interaction often leads to broader visibility. Recognize the difference between opinion and cut-and-dry misinformation.

- **Do we need to apologize?** Has the brand done something that will cause loss of brand affinity? Is an apology going to matter and be perceived as authentic? Can we deliver one without defending the actions?

- **Does the volume of comments or eyeballs require a response?** Sometimes even if it doesn't seem like a response will add value, the sheer size of the audience dictates a response. In these situations, just do your best to respond in a way that doesn't bring on yet more criticism later on.

- **Finally, a critical consideration:** If the crisis includes organized labor, include your legal team before taking any action. There are very specific rules that must be followed before a brand can comment. This is also good strategy when dealing with a political attack group.

Your Five-Step Response Plan for a High-Risk Issue

With many sensitive posts, next actions are often pretty straightforward—the questionable post or posts quickly get responses and life moves on. Sometimes a post can simply be removed; for example, if it's inappropriate material that violates the site's posting guidelines. (Those guidelines should be clearly posted on the About page or in another accessible place.)

For higher-level events, where research, discussion, and multi-party input are needed to plan a response, here's your action plan.

I. Stop or at least reconsider scheduled communications.

Sometimes a perfectly good ongoing content plan can seem inappropriate or insensitive when there's a crisis in play. Consider stopping scheduled social media posts and any paid social promotions. Be certain to check any tools used to schedule distribution to your social venues, removing scheduled posts.

Once the crisis is in hand, you'll want to turn your content engine back on, perhaps with some tweaks. Review any upcoming or newly scheduled content to ensure that it's unlikely to reignite negative chatter, and closely monitor new posts until the crisis is completely behind you.

2. Publish a pause post.

When you need time to consider the brand's response, publishing a "pause post" is one of the most effective ways to slow the flow of the conversation until you're ready. A pause post should be customized as much as possible and convey three distinct messages:

- We hear you and acknowledge your issue.

- We don't have an answer yet, but are working on one.

- You can expect an update by <time> on <site>.

For example: *Thanks, Shirley, for letting us know there was a problem with the customer service you experienced with your new Whozywhatzit 5Z. I've asked our team to investigate what happened and will come back to you with an update by 4:00 p.m. ET today on our blog <URL>.*

If the event discussion is all happening in a single space, it's relatively easy to share a pause post. If the event is viral across Facebook or Twitter, it is much more difficult—you'll have a lot of mouths to feed. But no matter how many pause posts you have to write, don't be robotic with responses. The way to be efficient isn't to post the same words to each person, but to pick the most influential people and respond only to them.

3. Decide where and when to respond.

If the issue is largely the complaint of a single person or group, consider taking an opportunity missed by so many companies: Get the customer or irate party on the phone! Talk with him or her one-on-one, starting with a simple prompt: "Please tell me what happened." Listen, take notes, and let the customer vent until he or she is finished. Then read back what you've recorded, so the customer knows you've listened, and let him or her know what the next step will be in getting the issue resolved. Then follow through! In the many crisis escalations we have handled for clients, this process rarely fails.

If the conversation has gone viral and crossed platforms, try to bring all the concerned customers back to a single point for the response and ensuing dialogue, if possible. A blog works well because it can be easily shared with a link and offers a consolidated space where readers can comment.

Ensure that the venue for the response matches the audience. If the negative backlash is, say, criticizing the behavior of a company executive and the chatter has all been on Twitter, product fans on a Facebook page probably will not be involved or interested. Go to the people who care.

Finally, consider the medium and the author: Written response? Video blog? Should the response be from "The Company," or is it a situation where personalizing the response makes it stronger?

4. Craft the response.

There's no super-secret formula here, but here are several best practices that I've seen contribute to a successful response.

- **Answer the question directly:** Don't dance around the issue. Fans and customers respond much better to the "we blew it" approach than to the "we're sorry if you felt bad" approach. It's OK to explain what happened, but only after clearly acknowledging what went wrong.

- **Be transparent and forthcoming:** Have you ever heard children try to explain why they misbehaved? That's how many brands sound to customers when they try to explain why they screwed up. Unless there are critical facts in error, don't start with the explanation, just apologize. Most companies don't get into real trouble unless they ignore an issue or try to talk their way out of it. Own it, take responsibility, and take the appropriate next step.

- **Be humble:** You (or whoever signs or says the apology) are not the all-powerful Oz in this moment, no matter how influential your brand. You are a human being standing in front of another human being to apologize. Ensure that your response conveys that level of humility and humanity. People understand that humans make errors. People forgive people, but they're not so accommodating of faceless corporate logos. (This is yet another reason why it's so important to use social to personalize your brand, in particular by bringing your people forward.)

- **Acknowledge their experience:** If someone has had a terrible experience, demonstrate your empathy by acknowledging the experience. You can be sincerely sorry, whether or not your company was responsible.

- **Read your response as a skeptic:** Find a voice of dissent on your team, read this person your composed apology, and ask for his or her most snarky response. You might be shocked at what you learn.

- **Be conversational, not robotic:** Select a voice and tone for the responses that will ease tensions, not add to them. Don't sound robotic or overly corporate. Be human. Address the person by name if possible, and sign the response from someone so it feels personal.

- **If the response is going to the masses, be sure to mix it up**: Make sure you are not copying and pasting the same response to each person involved. Basic content can be the same, but with variations to the language, greetings, etc.

5. Continue to follow up.

Posting the response is a good start to managing a crisis, but it's only the beginning. Continue to monitor and answer follow-up questions in the venue where the crisis occurred, but also look more broadly for new flare-ups. If you have centralized the discussion, provide readers with a link to the venue if they want to continue to follow it.

The media often becomes interested when a brand makes an official response. Make sure the PR team is ready and aligned on messaging when requests for comment come in. As industry bloggers start posting, read everything. Reach out to correct any incorrect coverage, and consider leaving positive comments from the brand on posts that do a good job analyzing the event and your response. Reach out directly to those bloggers as well—with thanks. The best thing you can do here is show you're taking all the learning you can from what happened. That shifts the story from "bad brand" to "improving brand."

Social in Action: Beware the Robot Voice

In August 2012, Progressive found itself in the spotlight after the brother of a girl who was killed in a wreck wrote a post on Tumblr called "My sister paid Progressive Insurance to defend her killer in court." The post went viral, and Progressive was mobbed with angry tweeters.

The company's response, apparently standard issue, came from its lawyers: "This is a tragic case, and our sympathies go out to Mr. Fisher and his family for the pain they've had to endure. We fully investigated this claim and relevant background, and feel we properly handled the claim within our contractual obligations."

Making it worse, they carbon copied the post to every negative responder, which made the company look even more apathetic. The response was so tone deaf that Wil Wheaton, the former *Star Trek* actor and popular blogger, ran Progressive's post through text-to-speech software and posted the audio with the note, "Dear Progressive Insurance PR Bot: This is what you sound like, you inhuman monster." More than 20,000 people listened to the recording.

The case offers two lessons for the rest of us.

1. The social web doesn't speak legalese. Legal input may be needed, or even required, particularly when a lawsuit is in play. But make sure to respond in natural, human language, with an emotional filter. If formal language is absolutely necessary, direct people to a static page rather than trying to have that conversation in social spaces.
2. You can't deliver a sincere message in the form of spam. By papering the web with one tone-deaf message, the company actually sent just one message: "We don't care enough to really listen."

Finally, gather the team for a post-crisis review to make sure your process, scripted responses, and business practices don't need to be updated with the lessons learned from this event. Consider creating an internal case study to ensure that your employee ambassadors have all the facts in the story and know how to de-escalate the next potential crisis.

A Four-Alarm Fire Isn't the Time to Make Friends

Although poor management can turn one complaining customer into a full-blown PR crisis, the very worst social crises are generally caused by a much deeper problem that reaches into the past, before the crisis began. Many companies leave themselves exposed by being reticent in developing their social presence. They don't see the need to plan for a social media crisis until after they are in the middle of one.

A company might think it's protecting itself by avoiding investing in a social presence. In fact, it's leaving itself as wide open as possible to the risks of social media, without gaining any of the benefits. Your customers don't need you to have a Facebook page—if they have something to say, they'll find a public forum to express it online. You can't hide.

When companies properly invest in social strategy, content, and moderation, they have an established voice, cultural context, and relationship with customers online. They have a clear, data-driven picture of who their customers are and where they can be reached. They are fluent in the tools and channels used to communicate in social—for example, they would be readily able to create and distribute an effective mea culpa message on the fly.

And most important, they have real, live brand representatives, who have cultivated relationships with ambassadors—those customers and industry folks who will support and defend the brand, or at least give it the benefit of the doubt. In other words, they've developed customers' *trust*.

These brand representatives could be in-house or from vendors. But they need to be social media–focused, experienced, and well trained. Being a member of the Facebook generation does not automatically mean an employee has social media–marketing and crisis management skills and expertise. Hanging out a social media shingle does not make a blogger or even a big, traditional marketing agency capable in this area.

But remember, nothing is more important to the lasting success of a brand than trust, and you can't build it during the heat of a crisis flashpoint. You don't first make friends in the middle of a crisis. You have to build those relationships ahead of time. If you've built trust, they are likely to give you the benefit of the doubt, so long as you listen, respect their concerns, and resist the urge to delete first and ask questions later.

Chapter 8 Key Takeaways:

✓ Have a crisis plan in place before a crisis hits.

✓ Never get defensive in a crisis; use the opportunity to listen and show customers you care.

✓ Research the issue carefully to prepare an informed response.

✓ Respond in a timely fashion, with a pause post if needed.

✓ Centralize the discussion on a single page to help slow its virality.

✓ Don't use legalese in social conversation.

✓ Don't blow the follow-up; make sure scheduled content is updated as needed.

✓ A long-term, successful social presence offers the best immunity when a crisis occurs. Build trusted relationships with brand ambassadors before a crisis hits.

Chapter 9:

Legal and Regulatory Issues, Oh My!

The dynamic free-for-all of social media understandably makes lawyers nervous. This chapter lays out the issues so that you can make informed decisions and mitigate risk.

"The wise man does not expose himself needlessly to danger."
—Aristotle

Navigating legal liability while participating in an unmediated, public conversation with customers can initially be a hair-raising proposition, particularly if you are working in a corporate or regulated environment. From my experience working with major brands in the most regulated industries in the world, I know that with proper planning and oversight, these challenges can be navigated. Our customers, even in pharma and finance, have thriving social platforms *and* sleep well at night.

This chapter shares the process and practices that companies in highly regulated or consumer-sensitive environments have used to succeed in social. The information here is useful not just for other regulated companies, but for any company looking to identify and mitigate the risk its social programs entail.

Making Friends with Legal

Protecting your company while getting your social program launched requires, first and foremost, that you build a strong into collaborative partnership with your legal team.

Here's a common scenario: A social media team develops the plan for an innovative new social program. They race enthusiastically toward the finish line, putting all of their energy into the many creative, technical, and logistical issues involved in designing a program and getting it online. Finally, it's just weeks or days before launch—or in some cases, even the day *after* launch—and suddenly someone remembers, "Oh yeah, all programs need legal approval." The program is then dropped in the laps of the lawyers as a near fait accompli.

How Legal Sees Marketing

How Marketing Sees Legal

Enter the company lawyers. They may not know much about social and aren't given much background about why the program is important or how the company will benefit. All they can see is exposure to new and uncertain risk, and a marketing department that doesn't seem to take the risk seriously or to have proactively managed the issues. Their own job is to protect the company from risk, including risks that shoot-from-the-hip employees haven't considered. All this translates to a quick no. In the case of one Fortune 20 brand, a $10 million campaign involving network television, print, packaging, digital, and social was brought to legal just three weeks before launch. Alas, neither the team nor the creative digital agency had considered that the centerpiece of the program, photos uploaded by customers, might need to be moderated. Legal shut this one down in seconds.

Meanwhile, companies in regulated environments have learned how to partner with legal not just to avoid a no, but to make a better program with fewer mistakes. Their industries are governed by strict rules about interactions with customers, and moving into social media requires a very careful look at how these rules apply.

To understand just how difficult it can be to operate in a regulated environment, consider this: If a fan posted, "I'm addicted to your lip balm" on a pharma brand's Facebook page, the company might be required to report it as an "adverse event" to the FDA. (The FDA considers "addicted" a very bad word.)

The most effective social media marketing managers partner with legal from the start. They realize that the lawyers need to be their best friends if social programs are going to survive and thrive.

Often the first answer from legal will be, "No, I don't think we can do that." But if marketing brings legal in early, explains their business goals and strategies, and then works hand in hand with their colleagues to understand the issues, the relationship very quickly becomes collaborative. They're able to work through what has to be done to manage and mitigate the risk.

Taking the time to educate your legal department about the goals and benefits of your social efforts creates a cooperative dynamic that allows them to see that potential risk exists against a backdrop of potential gain. Lawyers are there to protect the company, the brand, and, yes, the marketing managers too, by managing, mitigating, or eliminating legal risk. They know that the last is almost impossible, so they'll work with you to manage and mitigate, *if* you'll work with them. In this context good lawyers don't say no. They say, "OK, we have this managed. Now it's a business decision." They'll also tell your business superiors that you've planned accordingly and taken steps to make sure that any risk is calculated.

Educating the legal team often requires more than explaining the specific goals and strategies of your program. Take the time to teach them what you know about social and the potential benefits for the business. Walk them step-by-step through each platform, showing them how and why customers are using these tools. Be clear on the business goals and strategies. Show them what your competitors are up to. Filling any knowledge gaps makes it easier for them to do their job, and builds trust and a foundation for a solid partnership.

You Can Never Prepare Too Much

"You can never prepare too much" is a great rule of thumb for all brands as they move into social or launch new campaigns. As the legal counsel for one big brand has said, "You've got to work to anticipate what the consumers are going to do on your platform, the different routes. You may think you've got a fairly innocuous post. It could go five different ways. You need to think about those in advance. Have answers prepared."

The social media team at one of our pharma clients spent a full six months in advance of their launch working with their legal, medical, and regulatory departments to establish process and guidelines. Working with input from their brand teams, their care center, and LiveWorld, they created a database of thousands of posts and answers to different questions that could come up as users interacted in social. They really anticipated as much as possible. That kind of preparation doesn't eliminate risk, but it creates a structure that makes spontaneous interaction between customers and brands possible.

Planning the content calendar in advance allows plenty of time for review by all important stakeholders. Our pharma clients have calendars in place at least 60 days in advance. Once the calendars are planned, they're updated as needed to keep in tune with ongoing events and to keep the overall feel of the feed spontaneous and fresh.

Our clients' legal groups have told us that having an established system and process flow for creating and posting content, tools that track and archive content and actions, and an expert or trained moderation team (vendor or in-house) greatly improves social programs and substantially mitigates risk.

Moderating Content in Regulated Industries

It's safe to say that highly regulated brands often live and die by moderation. By moderation, I don't mean just monitoring or listening. I mean reviewing the content; thinking about it; and then acting on it in context by accepting it, rejecting it, or escalating it as appropriate.

Social in Action: Before a Campaign Launch, Wargaming

While some issues seem to emerge from nowhere, most companies and industries see certain complaints or issues recur over time and can use that to get a head start. Interview your PR team and customer contact centers for a list of potential flashpoints. A review of competitors' social pages might turn up still other issues to add to the list. For every identified hot issue, prepare and pre-vet responses so that they're on hand should the issue come up.

This type of preparation is sometimes called "wargaming"—and we at LiveWorld believe it's a best practice for all brands any time a new campaign or product is launched. It doesn't take long to pre-vet and wargame campaigns before they happen. The goal is figuring out how to handle scenarios from A to Z: What will we do if a live event goes down? If someone curses? If someone complains that the content or a celebrity tie-in doesn't match the brand's values or customer expectations?

You can definitely create canned responses in advance, but give the moderator or community manager enough leeway to customize the response to the situation. A post may be canned, but it can't *sound* canned—and the way to avoid that is having a wide set of responses ready to choose from, and also letting the poster make tweaks to personalize and adjust the cadence of the response.

For example, take a brand that posts or tweets about 50 times a day across a dozen pages, with each communication potentially generating hundreds of comments. Here monitoring the stream is a significant investment—but one that yields important marketing insights along with risk mitigation.

For any brand, quality moderation is one of the best tools, not just for managing risk, but for learning about customers and engaging them in a successful, lively conversation. Remember that your goal is not just to talk with your customers, but ultimately to get customers to talk with *each other*—a result that helps tremendously when you're trying to scale big, since it takes some of the content creation burden off of your team.

How much you decide to moderate depends on the brand itself, the brand's history, the regulatory environment, and any recent history of legal or PR issues.

Some brands use algorithms as their answer to the need for affordable 24/7 moderation. The trouble is, algorithms lack the human sensitivity and context awareness that make quality moderation possible. By "quality" I really mean four things: one, not letting guideline-violating comments slip through; two, not mistakenly rejecting positive comments; three, stepping into the conversation in a natural way that produces real engagement; and four, considering posts in their context before determining action. To expand on this last point, there are times when a seemingly problematic comment needs to be accepted. Suppose in the midst of a crisis the chief antagonist uses profanity that violates your guidelines. An algorithm would likely reject it. But a good moderator would consider the context and realize that rejecting the comment could make it seem to customers like the brand was trying to shut down criticism, leading to an escalation in the crisis.

It's for exactly this kind of sensitive scenario—and they come up all the time—that LiveWorld's moderation solution has a human moderator vetting every single comment. We use technology to make the humans better, faster, and more cost effective. That way we can let moderators spend most of their time contributing the elements that only humans can—conversing and connecting with other humans. (Besides which, people just don't like being managed by semantic algorithms.)

Not all brands need 24/7 attention to their social pages, but they all need a consistent, scalable plan for moderation. Anyone can handle a comment or two, but your goal is to have a lot of customers doing a lot of talking. How will you scale up when you have dozens or hundreds or thousands of comments per day or hour? How will you handle evenings and weekends, sudden spikes, and problem content? Consistency in how you moderate is incredibly important in building trust. It sets the tone and context for the way your customers will experience your brand online. Stay proactive by posting community rules and guidelines that make it clear to customers up front what principles underlie your moderation—if you do this, they will be much more cooperative and accepting when you need to police interactions. Shower attention on customers who behave as you want them to, and others will follow their example.

Also know the laws and the culture of your market segment. You can't moderate conversation successfully if you don't understand whom you're dealing with and in what context. For example, teenagers: when you're too restrictive in your interactions with teens, your brand's social presence will immediately become uncool and "fake," and they won't show up. But the definition of "restrictive" varies worldwide, in terms of both culture and law. France has extremely tight regulations, for example, on marketing content targeted at teenage girls. In the more liberal culture of the Netherlands, however, not only do you not have such laws, if you're too tight in your management your customers there won't pay you any attention. The better you know both your audience and the rules governing interactions—and, most important, the relevant cultural context—the better you'll be able to explore the range of interactions that are possible.

One final note on moderation: make sure that you empower your moderation team to be human. Although process and preparation are important, it's essential that the people talking directly with your customers have enough latitude to be present in their interactions and apply common sense and sensitivity, even when they're working from prepared content. Humans who act like robots aren't any better than actual robots in the eyes of the customer.

Educating Your Employees

Your company needs a social media policy so that employees, not just in marketing, but across the company, know what they can and can't say in social media. This is especially true in regulated environments, where common sense alone isn't enough to keep people from running afoul of industry-specific rules and requirements. And many companies in all industries are worried about confidentiality, given the ease of sharing and the potential virality of social content.

The problem I see with corporate social media policies in more relaxed industries is that they're often reflexively Draconian. They follow a command and control, punitive approach to managing employees that doesn't trust them to be capable caretakers of the company's interests. The truth is, if an employee is out to cause you harm in social media, he or she is not going to be stopped by your policy.

The more effective way to manage the risk of employees publishing in social is to create a participatory culture that celebrates them. Empower them with the knowledge that they're potentially the company's best, most effective representatives in social. Of course, that doesn't mean telling them that anyone can speak on behalf of the company to the press and analysts, or that social media is a license to violate confidentiality. So make sure they know to whom they should refer media inquiries. And make sure they understand the content of and reasons for your confidentiality policies. Don't just distribute a policy through email; give them real education and supportive guidelines.

The technology company Intel has an exemplary social media policy, which can be found on the Intel website. It's organized around three central principles, all of which are written in a way that shows the company respects the intent and intelligence of its employees:

1. **Disclose:** "Your honesty—or dishonesty—will be quickly noticed in the social media environment. Please represent Intel ethically and with integrity." The policy asks employees to be transparent, to be truthful, and to be themselves.

2. **Protect:** "Make sure all that transparency doesn't violate Intel's confidentiality or legal guidelines for commercial speech—or your own privacy. Remember, if you're online, you're on the record—everything on the Internet is public and searchable. And what you write is ultimately your responsibility."

3. **Use common sense:** "Perception is reality and in online social networks, the lines between public and private, personal and professional are blurred. Just by identifying yourself as an Intel employee, you are creating perceptions about your expertise and about Intel. Do us all proud."

However effective your policy and training, incidents will happen when employees are interacting in social media. But instead of resorting to extreme policies—for example, pre-screening any employee's remarks—emphasize and improve the guidelines and monitor the system to identify problems. When problems inevitably come up, it doesn't mean the approach is broken. It means incidents need to be resolved on a case-by-case basis.

It's also time we all got over the notion that when an employee or agency makes an honest mistake, it's time to fire the scapegoat. Customers understand that social media is fluid; mistakes happen. Acknowledging errors and treating your team appropriately is the mark of a people-oriented brand that can be trusted.

Privacy and Security in the World of User-Generated Content

The most important thing to be said here is this: communicate clearly and transparently how customer information and comments will be used. Again, planning helps, so that you know at the outset the ways you may want to use the content. You need people to opt in to those uses up front, or you'll find yourself stuck down the road.

Your company probably already has a privacy policy to protect customers—and if it was written before the advent of social media, it is probably out of date. For example, many big corporations have rules that require all user information to be encrypted so it can never be seen. That's pretty much at odds with business goals when, for example, you're operating a public community site or Facebook page and the whole point is for customers to see each other's comments.

The rules need to be rewritten, and it's up to you to lead the discussion in your company. When faced with resistance, remind your colleagues that your company can't opt out. You can't avoid social media simply because it creates new risks and concerns. Your competitors are there, or will be soon, and you're all faced with the challenge of creating guidelines for this new environment.

Work with your company's lawyers and technology security team to develop a new plan that's consistent with the values and risk profile of your company.

Don't Forget About Gut Checks

Inventor and SpaceX CEO Elon Musk once told *Wired* that he doesn't believe in process. "The problem is that at a lot of big companies, process becomes a substitute for thinking," he said.

I would say that when it comes to global brands communicating effectively in social, process is essential—but it should act in parallel with critical thinking, not be a substitute for it. A social media policy is there to support, not replace, the normal human vetting process. We have one client who uses what she calls the *New York Times* Rule: What will the consumers feel if they read about what you've done in the *New York Times*? Legal precedence is constantly shifting. In the end, what matters is whether consumers trust you.

Ultimately, addressing legal concerns isn't about playing it so safe that you never take a risk. It's about being thoughtful, considering the costs and the benefits, then moving forward with a thorough understanding of what could go wrong and what the consequences would be—or what attorney Gerry Stegmaier, a cyber-liability expert, calls "making mistakes on purpose."

As you consider both the goals and the risks of your social program, you shouldn't just be thinking about the immediate future. What does the situation look like six months or a year out? What would be the risks if the program needed to be scaled back? What does success look like? Asking these kinds of questions helps you shape expectations up front, both internally and with your fans. What is the long-term vision, and what are you looking to accomplish with that community, or that group, or that set of Pinterest boards—along with the objective short term?

Deepening the relationship with your customers through social has incredible benefits, in terms of increasing loyalty, gathering insights, and driving revenue. But it also raises the stakes—once you've connected in that environment, it can be damaging to go back. As the head of social and digital at one Fortune 50 company said, "Social isn't just for Christmas. It's for life." So make sure you're building sustainability into your program.

Chapter 9 Key Takeaways:

The most important steps to mitigate risk while embracing the dynamic interplay of conversations in social are to:

- ✓ Involve legal early and often.

- ✓ Be clear about goals so that risks can be balanced against benefits.

- ✓ Know that it's impossible to over-prepare.

- ✓ Educate stakeholders throughout your organization.

- ✓ Invest in quality moderation.

- ✓ Embrace risk, but manage it.

- ✓ Empower your team to be human.

- ✓ Develop a consistent, scalable plan for moderation.

- ✓ Plan for long-term sustainability.

Epilogue:
Adapt, Migrate, or Die

One of the primary themes I'd like you to take away from this book is the incredible power of creating value together with your customers that neither you nor they could generate alone. We often refer to co-creating with customers, but I hope you will think beyond even that. Today, social media has enabled a level of customer-driven business that transcends what management methodologies such as Six Sigma were able to imagine 20 or 30 years ago. Suddenly the distance between company and customer has been reduced to a mouse-click. Customer dialogue and relationships are literally at your fingertips.

Social media provides the space for your customers to connect and be creative, bringing everybody in your brand along for the ride. When you succeed in making an emotional connection among your customers, they bring you along and make you a part of their daily lives because they want to, not because you're bombarding them with brand messaging. They become your main marketing and sales channel. As social becomes more mature in your organization, the information you get from customers will allow you to improve your product and their experience of it. The reward for your brand is increased revenue, a competitive edge, higher quality, customer satisfaction, and lower costs.

But to experience those rewards, to truly *be social* beyond just the marketing function, most companies need a new operating manual, defining the brand experience as a cultural model that supports, includes, and is driven by customers. With this, companies need a new cultural dynamic internally as well—embraced by the entire team, led by you.

I call the winning cultural dynamic for the social era Inspire-Involve-Imagine (Triple-I). The old model, still the dominant one, is Command-Control-Compliance (Triple-C). Making the shift has sweeping implications throughout an organization, but those companies that do will move beyond just being customer centric to being customer involved. These will be the most innovative and competitive brands.

By weaving the principles of social that I've described in this book into your team's DNA, you'll be taking your first great leap toward becoming a Triple-I company.

Which Are You Today?

Triple-C companies and their marketing departments follow a cultural model of command, control, and compliance. Brand messaging is created from the top down and broadcast out through both traditional marketing and social media channels. Brands talk *at* customers, essentially telling them to identify and act on a brand-centric, broadcast message. Employees are controlled as far as what to think and say when interacting with customers. The company-customer interaction runs through a narrow funnel made up of the marketing, sales, and service departments.

Meanwhile, companies that learn to truly embrace and leverage social orchestrate but do not control the message or the channels, nor do they even attempt to control their customers. They are governed by the Triple-I model. Through an ongoing dialogue, they *inspire* customers to *imagine*—to co-create an ever-evolving socialized brand experience, which shifts the relationship first from broadcast to engagement, and ultimately to *involvement:* an active emotional dialogue *among* and with the customers that develops a commitment to the brand. This new model also guides employee relationships. Every employee becomes a potential brand representative, and the brand provides guidance and tools to inspire and facilitate their ambassadorship. After all, doesn't every company want its brand and its employees to know and get close to the customer?

Ideally, this isn't just about adjusting your existing process to allow for some social interference; taking that approach limits your success. Shifting to the Triple-I model is really about upending the way you've traditionally done things, from product development to marketing, to allow customer dialogue and relationships to drive the process. It's about recognizing that to swim in social, your marketing team can't control the message—and even if they could, they shouldn't want to.

Aspiring to Triple-I

Depending on your business, at this time you may be able to cede only so much control to your customers and employees. You may be in a regulated industry (pharma, finance) or have a legal department that's not quite ready for this. You may have internal institutional barriers; leaders who were comfortable and safe in the Triple-C world may not be ready to let go of the old way. But you can go in steps, and even aspiring to move in the direction of inspire, involve, and imagine means you've got one foot in the new model.

But it's time to take those steps—to, as Dr. Crouch, my eighth-grade biology teacher, said on our first day of class, "adapt, migrate, or die." One of the great (and most challenging) realities of the Internet is that the best practice anywhere quickly becomes the best practice expected by users everywhere. A great example is Amazon's 1-Click: Customers love it, and assume that because one company can make it happen on the webpage in front of them, all other companies should be able to do so as well. That's not immediately or easily possible for most sites, but the customers don't care. Amazon's best practice has set the bar for everyone else.

The same applies in social. That means that as soon as one brand in your space moves to Triple-I, putting the customer dialogue and relationships in the driver's seat, not just with marketing but with everything it does, your customers will expect you to as well.

In 2014, as I finished this book, LiveWorld had its 18th anniversary. When I think about how much the company has changed in those 18 years—and how much the marketing world has changed—I'm amazed. Reinvention for companies is never easy; you can barely turn a surfboard on a dime, let alone an ocean liner. And yet LiveWorld, like any company that's been around for more than one bubble, has risen and fallen and reinvented itself again and again. But for us it was never a total reinvention. Through it all, our founding vision never changed: we help companies create transformative relationships through online dialogue, enabling people to create value together that they could not create by themselves.

I can't help but think that we might not have succeeded but for our founding mission. As a relationship-based company, we have always been more prepared than most to make those great and difficult pivots when they've been necessary. Our mission and the culture that grew from it gave us the tools we needed—high-trust relationships that naturally fit the Triple-I model—to reinvent ourselves as times have changed.

That's good news for all of you who are starting down the road to deepen relationships and shift to Triple-I. By taking your first steps into social as a company, deepening relationships with customers and within your team, you're tightening the bolts to prepare yourself not just for the present social era, but for all the radical pivots ahead.

In some ways, it's especially good news for those of you who are at companies where co-creating and implementing a Triple-I model are new and difficult processes. You have the biggest potential gains.

I hope this book helps you begin to experience the exciting potential of social media to transform your company, your team, and your customers—together.

Appendix:
The Social Media Toolkit

Facebook

World's largest social networking service, centered on user (and brand) pages, and on sharing comments and photos with lists of friends

Big audience potential

Multimedia—
video, photos,
interactive apps

Offline component—
events, check-ins, deals

Threaded
conversations

Robust
advertising platform

Real people with mostly
symmetrical relationships

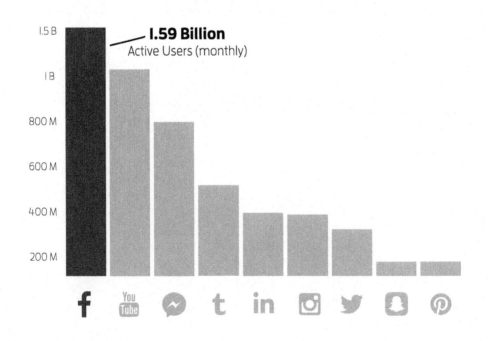

1.59 Billion
Active Users (monthly)

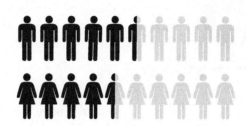

55% **MALE**

45% **FEMALE**

Facebook users ages 18+ Spend

7.3
hours
per month

on Facebook's mobile site

I in 4 Facebook users

check their account **5** or more times daily

Facebook accounts for
I in every 5
page views on the web

Messenger

Instant mobile messaging and chat app integrated with Facebook that allows embedded photos and video. Messenger is expected to become a full platform for apps, commerce, and customer service.

#1 activity

9.5 billion photos sent through Messenger every month

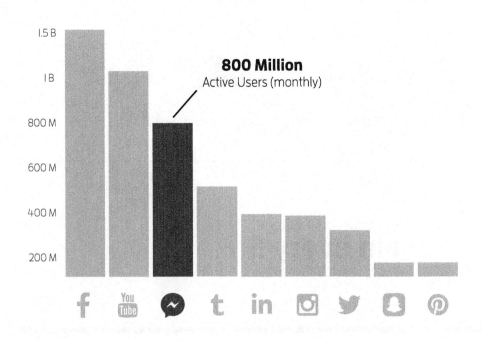

800 Million
Active Users (monthly)

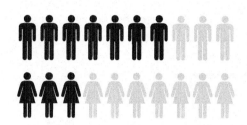

70% MALE

30% FEMALE

Facebook is testing US-based **e-commerce options** for Messenger, including direct sales capabilities

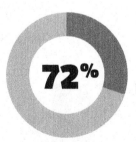

72%

of Facebook Messenger users purchase products online

Source: DMR Digital Stats, Facebook, Fast Company

Platforms at a Glance

Instagram
Social networking service focused on taking pictures or videos on mobile phones and sharing them

Highly mobile | Creative and playful | Selfies

Location-based | Tagged and searchable

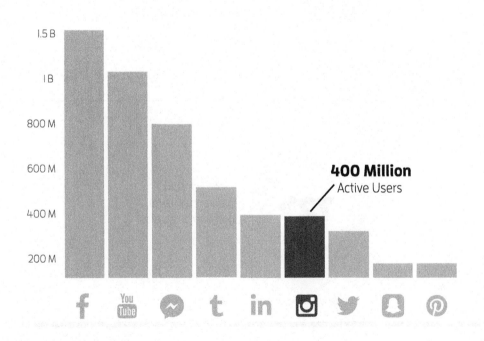

400 Million
Active Users

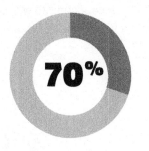

Percentage of users
that log in at least
once a day

70%

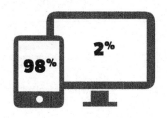

Percentage of time spent on
mobile app vs. desktop

98%   2%

200,000 brands advertise on Instagram
75% are outside of the U.S.

80 Million Photos posted
per day

3.5 billion Likes daily

LinkedIn

Business-oriented social networking site with a strong member directory function used by professionals for networking

Business to business

Professional networking

Increasingly focused on the newsfeed

Symmetrical relationships

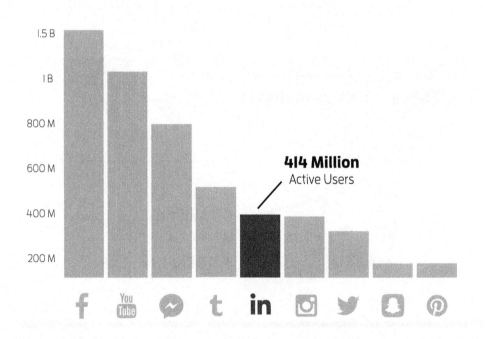

414 Million
Active Users

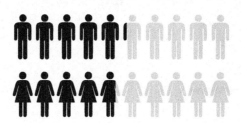

53% MALE

47% FEMALE

Every **2** seconds someone joins LinkedIn

Ages of users

More than 40 million students and recent college graduates use LinkedIn, comprising the platform's fastest growing demographic

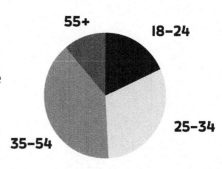

55+

18–24

25–34

35–54

The average household income of LinkedIn users is

$109,000

Sources: Inqbation, soshable, mediabistro

131

Pinterest

Online social scrapbooking service, centered on collections of photos tied to interests or projects

Visual

Self-branded identities

Aspirations, interests, and hobbies

Heavily skewed female
(fashion, beauty, weddings, gifts)

Topic based

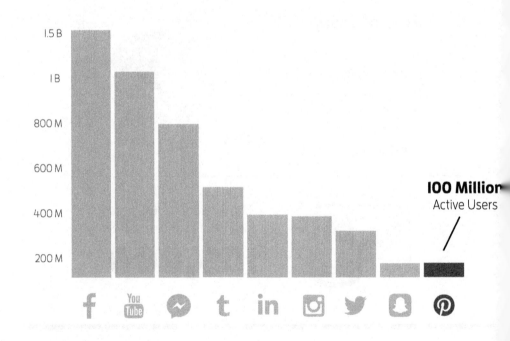

100 Million
Active Users

32%
MALE

68%
FEMALE

50%
of US moms who use Pinterest would follow a brand if rewards were offered to them

93%
of Pinners have used Pinterest to plan for or make purchases

Source: Millward Brown, 2015

The average household income of Pinterest users is

$100,000

Sources: ReadWrite, Mashable, Dazeinfo.com, omnicore, Business2Community

133

Tumblr
Microblogging platform and social networking website; users post multimedia and other content to short-form blogs

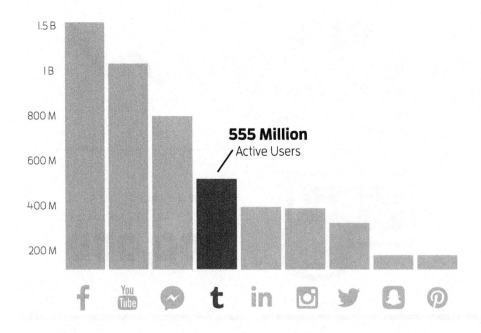

555 Million
Active Users

50%
MALE

50%
FEMALE

42%

of all activity happens
from 5:00 p.m. to 1:00 a.m.

59%

of users under
the age of 29

Sources: Tumblr, Union Metrics, Expanded Rambings, Pew, Business Insider

Twitter

Social networking and microblogging service that enables users to send and view 140-character text messages, images, and video

Brevity

Tagged conversations— hashtags make it easy to find/track info

Trends—organic and paid

Discovery—people can find like-minded people and topics of interest

Real people with mostly symmetrical relationships

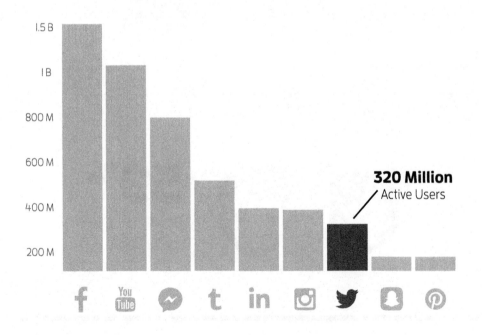

320 Million Active Users

500,000
Tweets sent per day

At 140 characters, that's over 130,000 King James Bibles.
Stacked atop each other, the stack would be over 3 miles high.

80%
of all twitter
users

access Twitter via mobile

Integrated with Periscope
LiveStreaming

What makes
you retweet?

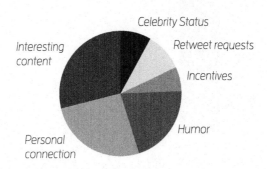

Interesting
content

Celebrity Status

Retweet requests

Incentives

Humor

Personal
connection

Sources: Infographiclabs.com and jeffbullas.com, infographicsinspiration.com, ansonalex.com

YouTube
Video-sharing website

Every day people watch **hundreds of millions** of hours of video, generating billions of views

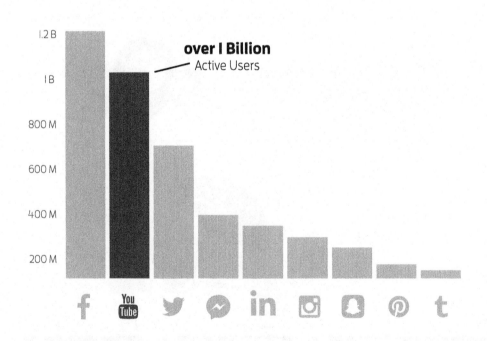

over I Billion
Active Users

YouTube on mobile alone reaches more 18-34 and 18-49 year-olds **than any US cable network**

Online video accounts for  **50%** of all mobile traffic

Every minute **100** hours of video are uploaded to YouTube

World's **second-largest** search engine

500 **years** of YouTube video are watched **daily** via Facebook

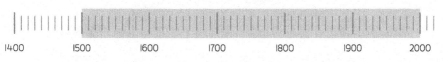

| 1400 | 1500 | 1600 | 1700 | 1800 | 1900 | 2000 |

Sources: dreamgrow.com, flowtown, customerinsightgroup.com, viralblog.com

139

Snapchat

Snapchat is a messaging platform for text, labeled images, and videos compiled into "stories" with a brief 24-hour shelf life. Snapchat holds a high appeal for Millennials; 71% of users are under 34 years old.

1-to-1 and group messaging platform

"Private" sharing; stories expire in 24 hours

Image and video sharing predominate

Geotargeted campaigns and stickers

"Discover" features curated selection of media sources and brands

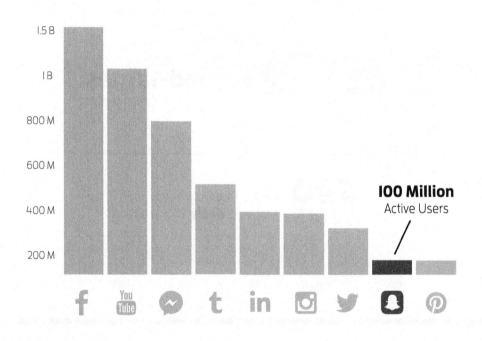

100 Million
Active Users

The IT Department

When IT Says:

"We'd rather you not use 3rd-party platforms."

You Say:
"The social media industry is changing how we do business; we have to change, or we'll be left behind. We have to work with third-party environments because that's where our customers are. I'm here so that we can figure out the risks and the complications together."

What They're Thinking:
IT departments create process and protocol that make it possible to deliver consistent, supportable technology solutions across a company. That predisposes them, naturally, to want a certain amount of control over how your people are using technology to do business and gather information about customers. Once "application *x*" becomes essential to workflow, any problems that come up become IT's responsibility to manage. They're also looking to limit the company's potential liability from technology or security failure. These are real concerns not to be taken cavalierly. Often IT's standard processes, platforms, and rules have been developed with a focus on either internal enterprise applications or the management of highly sensitive customer data, such as credit card and social security numbers. Working with IT to help them understand the kinds of information being shared in social media makes them a partner in finding appropriate solutions and, when needed, sunsetting rules that don't apply.

The Follow-Up:
1. Lay out your business objectives and explain the context of open social media networks, in which consumers participate because they want to share information with others. Explain how the platform/application/tool is meeting your objectives.

2. Work with IT to evaluate your proposal relative to their parameters, and their parameters relative to the social context and your business objectives.

3. Identify potential risks to security or existing IT practices. Case by case, decide which risks have worthwhile trade-offs, and which can be mitigated or avoided altogether.

How to Talk to...

Your CEO

When Your CEO Says:

"I'm not ready to spend so much on something with unproven ROI— especially when all I hear you say is 'relationships' not 'sales.'"

You Say:
"Conversation and relationships lead to sales."

"Our customers act in real time, so we need to market in real time."

"We always say we want to get closer to our customers. This gives us a way to do it."

"Ninety-three percent of Americans say companies should have a social media presence; 85 percent believe companies should go further than just having a presence on social sites and should interact with their consumers." (Source: Cone Business in Social Media Study)

"The companies showing the best success in social media spend two times more than everyone else—but are four times more successful." (Source: Tata Consultancy Services)

What He or She Is Thinking:
Your CEO is focused on leveraging resources to generate revenue, and is often under pressure to produce short-term financial results. He or she may not understand that the power of social media is in building deeper relationships that convert occasional and lower-revenue buyers into lifelong, higher-revenue customers, who spend more and recommend your company to others.

The Follow-Up:

1. Present your CEO with case studies that show how companies have successfully driven sustained revenue growth through social campaigns.

2. Build ROI models, such as customer acquisition, that demonstrate business value of social without needing to tie it directly to sales.

3. Show the cost savings your social program versus traditional ad buys using a marketing equivalency calculation.

4. Show your CEO both negative and positive comments the brand has received on social media, without the company's involvement. This points at both the risk of not getting involved and the opportunity of doing so.

How to Talk to...

Your Social Media Intern

When Your Social Media Intern Says:

"We really just have to do it my way, even if it doesn't seem to make marketing sense or meet business goals. After all, I am the expert in social media."

You Say:
"Here's a pre-paid SIM card. Call your mother and tell her you are not ready for a grown-up job." (I'm paraphrasing a great movie, *The Paper Chase.*)

OK, don't really say that. After all, you hired the intern to help him or her learn and grow, and to bring a youthful—and yes, socially savvy—perspective.

What you really say is this:

"We think social media is great. After all, that's why you are here. But we are first and foremost a business that needs to meet business goals. That's why we are all here. And we have quite a few people whose approval of and investment in our social program are necessary for its success. They don't understand social so much and are not going to help if we're not clear on how this helps meet our business goals.

"So: Tell me your thoughts on our social brand identity, optimal conversational content topic mix, social crisis management, and social ROI models? Not sure what I'm talking about? I'll tell you, and then let's review our business goals, how marketing really works to meet goals, and your ideas on how social media can work to do that too."

(You don't have to tell him or her you learned about all of these in this book.)

What He or She Is Thinking:
Interns are enthusiastic about social media and excited to have been hired by your company to help with it. But they don't know yet what they don't know about business and marketing. Most likely they've never been in a large corporation where the organizational dynamics can make or break a program. And they probably don't realize that there are now a lot of middle- and senior-level people who are experienced in social media. Your social media intern may not even realize that social media is fundamentally relationship marketing.

The Follow-Up:
1. Send the intern out to interview your key stakeholders on their goals, what they know about social media, and what they think about it.

2. Have the intern prepare a social media plan that starts with the business goals you've laid out, then works through the intern's creative ideas and ties them back to the goals.

3. Iterate the plan with the intern so he or she learns a lot about business and marketing, and you learn what he knows about social media.

4. Give the intern a copy of this book.

How to Talk to...
A False Social Media Expert

When a False Social Media Expert Says:

"I know all about this and can help you meet your social media goals and solve your problems."

You Say:
"Just a few questions first: How many years of actual experience do you have in this space, conceiving and executing social media programs for clients? Not just creating ads or posting content, but working through business goals and content plans, and then seeing the program through?

"Give me some examples of the programs you've created. What were the goals, the metrics, and the results? What worked? What didn't work? (Anyone who can't discuss what didn't work hasn't really worked in social media.)

"Give me your thoughts on optimal conversational content mix, social ROI models, and social crisis management."

What He or She Is Thinking:
False experts think that traditional marketing experience in itself qualifies them for social media consulting. Or they think their own personal use of social media qualifies them as social media marketing experts, prepared to work with clients in large, complicated organizations.

The Follow-Up:
1. If he or she doesn't answer your questions satisfactorily, decline his or her services.

145

An Internet Minute

48,000+
Apps downloaded

3.1 million
Facebook Likes/shares

4.1 million
searches

38,000
photos uploaded

1 Minute

500+
websites created

$430,000
spent online

100 hours of
video uploaded

347,000
tweets sent

Consumer Trust in Types of Advertising and Promotion*
% rating 4 or 5 on a scale of 1 (do not trust at all) to 5 (trust completely)

Brand or product recommendations

Professionally written online reviews

Consumer-written online reviews

Natural search engine results

Information on websites of companies or brands

Sponsored search engine reults

Emails from companies or brands

Posts by companies or brands on social networking sites

Information on mobile applications from companies or brands

Ads on websites (e.g., banners)

Text messages from companies or brands

■ US
■ EU

0   10%   20%   30%   40%   50%   60%   70%   80%

Based on 60K US and 15K EU responses in a study conducted by Forrester

Source: Forrester

147

Regional Social Media Use[*]

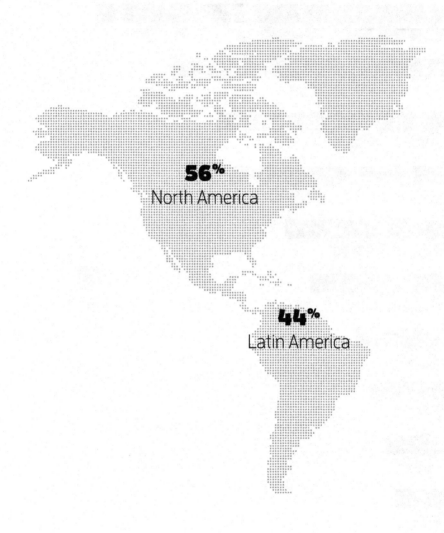

56%
North America

44%
Latin America

44%
Western Europe

43%
East Asia

24%
Middle East

26%
Southeast Asia

44%
Australia/Oceania

By % of population based on active users of the most active social network in each country
Source: We Are Social

Persuasive Charts and Graphs

Social Media Users: Distribution by Age

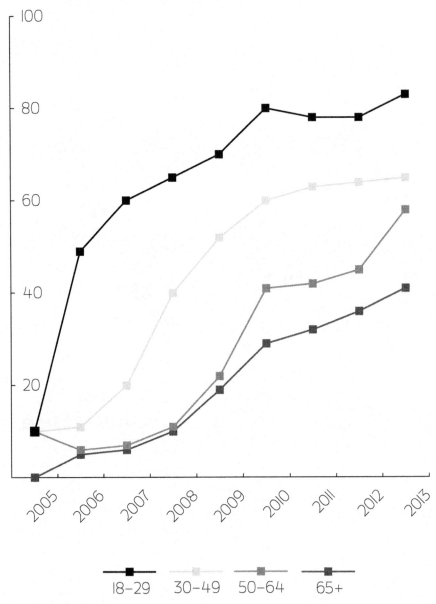

Source: Pew Center's Internet & American Life Project surveys: February 2005, August 2006, May 2008, April 2009, May 2010, May 2011, December 2012, and December 2013

Purchase Behaviors

Social commerce forecasts
$30 billion in 2015

78% of Americans say their purchases
are influenced by social media

47% of Americans say Facebook is their
#1 influencer of purchases

40% of Twitter users regularly search
for products via Twitter

12% of consumers have purchased
a product found on Twitter

Some **167 million** people will shop online this year
(192 million by 2016), spending an average
of $1,800 per person per year

Sources: The Social Skinny, Forbes

Persuasive Charts and Graphs

Facebook ROI: The Value of a Fan

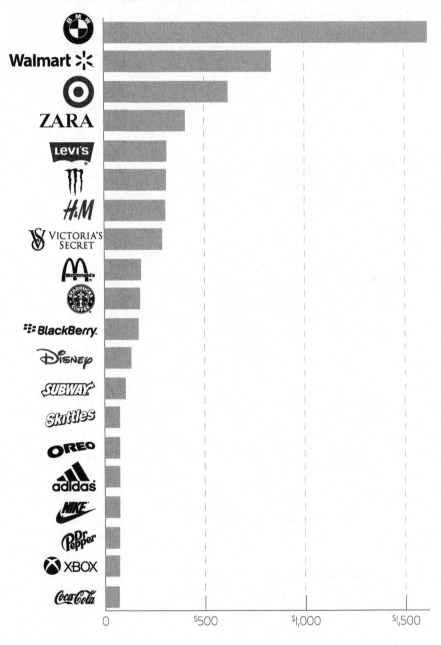

Source: Syncapse 2013

Social Brand Dynamic Exercise

When "I, your customer," encounter the brand through my social networks…

- ❸ Who is the brand to me?
- ❸ How does the brand empower my network of associates and friends?
- ❸ What should I tell my associates about you? What will they tell me?

Social Brand Identity: Creating a Sense of Place Where Culture Thrives

This chart, a companion to chapter 4, Socialize the Brand, is an exercise to help you establish your social brand identity and guide its development through conversation in your social spaces.

Socialized brand	One-line statement of identity? What kind of party are we giving?
Identity of the community	The social experience?
Purpose	How will people know what the community is about and how to act as members? Should there be an acculturation process or path?
Style	Will it be informal and loose? Hip, with "attitude"? Business like?
Content	What are the primary content and purpose for our community? The core unit of exchange? (E.g., recipes, reviews, technical questions/answers, social conversation around shared enthusiasms, and so on.)
Differentiation	How is our community different from or similar to others? What are the attributes that need to come across to its users?
Membership	Is everyone welcome to view and participate, or are we looking for selective membership or earned involvement?
Role models	Who will help us set the environment by "living" in the community and providing a model as a host or facilitator? Or, if we don't intend to have such a role, how will we set the pace?
Leadership	Who's our ideal participant in this community? If we don't have a host, how will we encourage leaders to arise?
Recognition	How will members get recognition or status?
Resources	Do we have resources and plans to provide incentives to participate?

Content Resources

Crafting Your Brand Story

1. What are your strategic objectives? (Transaction, engagement, awareness, education, rebranding?)

2. How will you use social to fulfill the objectives? (Customer benefits: self-expression, connection, or attention?)

3. How will you measure success? (KPIs?)

4. Whose voice tells the story? (POV: The customer, the brand, a blend of both, or an outside party?)

5. Describe the characters in your brand story. Who is the star, and who plays supporting roles? (See Detailed Character Description.)

6. What problem does your brand solve for your customers? (Character objectives: Am I special? Am I good or bad? Am I beautiful? Smart? Safe? In control of life?)

7. What challenges to their needs and wants do your customers face—in other words, what are the character obstacles in your story?

8. Which social channel(s) will you use to tell and amplify your story—and why? (Facebook, Twitter, Pinterest, Instagram, LinkedIn, etc.)

9. How does the story begin, and how will you keep it going? (How frequently will you update the story?)

10. How does the story end?

Developing Customer Profiles

Profiling your primary customer groups is a first step to improving your social content and preparing to bring customers into your storytelling. Get started with our worksheets.

Name: _____

Age: _____

Gender: _____

Marital status: _____

Children: _____
(number and ages)

Location: _____
(rural, small town, medium, urban)

Three adjectives to describe this group: _____

What do they want? _____

What size role do they play in the story? _____
(% of customer base)

Name: _____

Age: _____

Gender: _____

Marital status: _____

Children: _____
(number and ages)

Location: _____
(rural, small town, medium, urban)

Three adjectives to describe this group: _____

What do they want? _____

What size role do they play in the story? _____
(% of customer base)

Name: _____

Age: _____

Gender: _____

Marital status: _____

Children: _____
(number and ages)

Location: _____
(rural, small town, medium, urban)

Three adjectives to describe this group: _____

What do they want? _____

What size role do they play in the story? _____

(% of customer base)

Detailed Character Description

During this exercise, feel free to get creative as you use the worksheet to help draw a character sketch based on your customer profile. Fill out once for each persona, including your brand.

Character profile: _____

Photo:
Find a photo or illustration to represent each persona

Name: _____

Age/sex/location: _____

Education: _____

Occupation: _____

Responsibilities: _____

Likes about job or home life: _____

Dislikes about job or home life: _____

Frustrations: _____

Concerns: _____

Customer for how long: _____

Needs: _____

Wants: _____

Role in buying process: _____
(decider, user, gatekeeper, adviser)

Motivation to buy: _____

Social channels used and experience in channel: _____

Optimal social times: _____
(times when online)

Developing Business Objectives

1. **Business Objectives:** Rank each by percentage of priority.

    • Brand awareness: _____

    • Transactions: _____
    (sales, registrations, promo codes, etc.)

    • Engagement: _____
    (customer feedback, ideation)

    • Education: _____
    (downloads, product info)

    • Learning: _____
    (customer needs/wants, product feedback, competitor info)

2. **KPIs**: How will you know your effect on the audience? Pick two to three KPIs for each strategic objective and your target.

Objective	KPI #1	Goal	KPI #2	Goal	KPI #3	Goal
Brand awareness						
Transactions						
Engagement						
Education						
Learning						

3. **Business Strategies:** How do you hope to achieve selling more product, earning more market share, share of voice, etc.? Goals can be broad or very specific.

    • Objective (sample): Increase market share among single females 18–34.

    • Objective (sample): Increase share of Hispanic market.

    • Objective (sample): Be the most authentic brand in our industry.

4. **Applying KPIs to Objectives:** How will you know when you have reached your objectives? Pick two to three KPIs for each business objective and your target.

Objective	KPI #1	Goal	KPI #2	Goal	KPI #3	Goal
Increase market share women 18–24	Engagement rates	Increase engagement from 8% to 12% on FB	Share of voice	Positive mention by 3–4 key influencers	Sales revenue	Increase sales to group by 5%

5. **Tactical Objectives :** What will you do in social to support your business objectives, and how will those efforts benefit your customer? (Check against your customer profiles, and their wants and needs.)

Objective #1: Tactical, Creative Brainstorm (Increase market share among 18–24 female)

Idea 1: _____

Customer benefit: _____

Idea 2: _____

Customer benefit: _____

Objective #2: Tactical Brainstorm

Idea 1: _____

Customer benefit: _____

Idea 2: _____

Customer benefit: _____

Objective #3: Tactical Brainstorm

Idea 1: _____

Customer benefit: _____

Idea 2: _____

Customer benefit: _____

Optimizing the Channel Mix: Strengths and Opportunities

	Strongest Target Audience	Best Use	Ecosystem	Keys for Success
f	Women, 18- to 29-year-olds, families, consumer (not brand).	Connecting with friends, people who already know and like you.	Entertain me. See me. Give me something. Why should I pay attention to you?	Fun, coupons, humor, stories, informative, personal.
Twitter	18- to 29-year-olds, African Americans, urban residents.	Creating new relationships.	Be useful, talk about others, share resources.	Links, info, 1-to-1 contact, establish expertise.
in	35 and above, professional, high-income earners.	Professional networking and best practice sharing.	Give business value and contacts.	Share valuable content, join discussions, career networking.
YouTube	18–29, heavy mobile users, consumer (not brands).	Reach, branding, information, repository of video assets.	People look for good content to share and LOVE to share links and comments.	Short and entertaining is best, but good for long form too.
Snapchat	13–34, mobile, celebrity/media/ connecting interests.	Timely stories and promotions, humorous content.	Entertain me. Show me something worth sharing.	Memetic humor, current trends, 1-to-1 connection.
Messenger	Women and men, highest usage among 18-44 demographic.	Customer service: private chat ideal for PII sharing (orders, contact info, photos)	People who need 1-to-1 help, "I have a question."	Responsiveness, deference, allowing "opt-in."

Optimizing the Channel Mix: Limitations and Challenges

	Channel Limitations	Challenges	How to Fail
f	Needs promotion & advertising to drive new connections and content receipt.	Difficult to engage with low number of fans, growth is slow if organic.	Talk mostly about the brand or brand products.
(Twitter)	Tough to cut through the noise to make new relationships.	Must FIND people to engage.	Talk only about the brand or products.
in	Many users only participate by posting their resume.	Overrun with businesses spamming their content. Hard to differentiate.	Spam content with little business and engagement value.
You Tube	It's visual only, must have video assets in order to play.	Time-intensive and costly creation and outreach.	Comment spam, uninteresting videos.
(Snapchat)	Stories "expire" in one day.	Gaining followers and engaging younger, media-savvy audiences.	Post dull or dated content, hard sell with low value.
(Messenger)	Delays in brand replies are amplified by expectations in instant texting environment	Customers may be distracted by other activities. Do poeple trust Facebook Messenger to keep details private?	Be intrusive. Unsolicited outreach via text can seem "creepy."

Social Crisis Checklist

When dealing with a potential land mine, use this checklist to determine the threat assessment and develop a response.

1. **Understanding the story**
   - ✓ Who is the originator of the issue?

   - ✓ What is his or her motivation?

   - ✓ Is this a known adversary?

   - ✓ Has this person found a history of issues similar to his or hers?

   - ✓ What is his or her relationship to the brand/company?

Now that you have a better picture of the story behind the post, it is important to step back and look at the potential risk of the situation.

2. **Evaluating Brand Risk**
   - ✓ How influential are the people discussing the topic?

   - ✓ Is the conversation volume growing or declining?

   - ✓ What outreach options do you have?

   - ✓ What is the potential for public outrage?

   - ✓ Is the topic high risk?

Sample Threat Assessment Guide

Risk Level	Description	Examples
Low	A series of complaints or issues that begins to look like a trend. OR A single brand mention or issue that has a story with significant gravity and outrage that may cause it to spread rapidly. OR A social crisis that is arising within the brand's industry or product space that has the potential to spread to your brand.	Complaints about an advertising campaign not being sensitive to a group A story of gross misbehavior by an employee or grievous injury from a product A competitor's involvement in a social crisis based on a product characteristic that your product shares
Medium	Repetitive posts on a single topic in a set time period and with a certain passion level. OR A concern that is gaining momentum and following on a single or on multiple social channels.	Similar to low level, but with larger visibility and higher post levels
High	An explosive volume of comments on an individual subject or related topics with high passion levels. The content or audience is aggressively growing. There is usually a high-risk topic with high momentum and high spread often, to various channels (Facebook, Twitter, blog, etc.).	Major company and product events or issues Issues that drive public outrage generally include a perception of injustice that is being viewed by a high-level audience

163

Sample Contact List by Crisis Level

	Low	Medium	High
Business Team	**Owner: Business Level Project Manager** Name Phone number Email Backup **Commitment level:** *Required*	**Owner: Business Level Project Manager** Name Phone number Email Backup **Commitment level:** *Required*	**Owner: Business Level Project Manager** Name Phone number Email Backup **Commitment level:** *Required*
	Additional Business Team members: Name Phone number Email Backup **Commitment level:** *Optional/required*	**Additional Business Team members:** Name Phone number Email Backup **Commitment level:** *Optional/required*	**Additional Business Team members:** Name Phone number Email Backup **Commitment level:** *Optional/required*
Social Media Team	**Social Media Lead** Name Phone number Email Backup **Commitment level:** *Required*	**Social Media Lead** Name Phone number Email Backup **Commitment level:** *Required*	**Social Media Lead** Name Phone number Email Backup **Commitment level:** *Required*
	Additional Business Team members: Name Phone number Email Backup **Commitment level:** *Optional/required*	**Additional Business Team members:** Name Phone number Email Backup **Commitment level:** *Optional/required*	**Additional Business Team members:** Name Phone number Email Backup **Commitment level:** *Optional/required*
Subject Matter Expert (SME)	*Optional based on issue needs*	*Optional based on issue needs*	*Required for issue input)*

PR/ Communi- cations	*Optional based on issue needs*	*Optional based on issue needs*	**Assigned PR Member** Name Phone Number Email Backup **Commitment Level:** *Required* **Additional Team Members:** Name Phone Number Email Backup **Commitment Level:** *Optional/required*
Legal/ Regulatory	*Optional based on issue needs*	*Optional based on issue needs* **Assigned contact** Name Phone number Email Backup **Commitment level:** *Optional*	**Assigned Member** Name Phone Number Email Backup **Commitment Level:** *Required* **Additional Team Member:** Name Phone Number Email Backup **Commitment Level:** *Optional/required*
Response Goal	2–4 hours for initial response	I–2 hours for initial response	I–2 hours for initial response

The Social Media Lexicon from A to Z

Algorithm: A mathematical formula in software that allows computers, applications, and websites to perform their tasks. This term is most commonly mentioned in social media when referring to Facebook's and Google's algorithms, which prioritize distribution of content from brands to users and among users.

Animated GIF (Graphics Interchange Format): These used to be most commonly seen making graphics in banner ads move, but these days the most common GIFs seen in social are short video clips that loop endlessly, often to humorous effect.

API (Application Programming Interface): An API allows one software application to interact with another. APIs allow content to be shared between different applications—for example, the Facebook API allows Instagram to offer cross-posting to the Facebook channel.

Avatar: An image that represents a user to others in an online community. It can be user submitted or a default assigned by the community.

Bitly: One of many free URL-shortening services that crunches down longer URLs for easier social sharing; also allows content makers to track their links as they're shared throughout the social web. Often used on Twitter to enable a comment and a URL to fit within 140 characters.

Chat: Text-based, real-time conversation online; can be one-to-one or among a group of individuals.

Circles: Google+ terminology for user-created friend groupings that allow users to control who sees what of the content they share in the channel.

Comments: Responses to posts on blogs or social networks. Comment counts have traditionally provided a rudimentary engagement metric for social posts.

Community Manager: Community managers act as party planners, hosts, and/or DJs for your online social media party. Managers start and encourage conversations, acclimatize new users to the community, introduce members to each other, and ensure that the site's social brand identity develops in a way that resonates with and supports both the brand and the target users.

Connections: On the professional networking site LinkedIn, terminology used in place of "friends" to distinguish the B2B environment.

Content: A catch-all term to describe prepared text, pictures, and video created for sharing on the Internet. "Content" could describe something as simple as social media status updates or as developed as a full-length e-book.

Content Management System (CMS): An application that gives nontechnical people, such as editors or community managers, the ability to create and manipulate content for websites. Third-party CMSs, such as Joomla and WordPress, are becoming increasingly popular even for major brands, but traditionally many companies have developed custom CMSs.

Crowdfunding: Raising money to launch creative projects, products, cause campaigns, and businesses. This can be done on Kickstarter, IndieGogo, Cause, and a number of other websites.

Crowdsourcing: Gathering information or making decisions by calling upon members of a social community or people at large to contribute ideas, intelligence, and opinions. Crowdsourcing is an excellent way to engage a community.

Direct Messaging: Private, one-to-one messaging on social networks and community sites. *Direct Message,* a.k.a. *DM,* is specifically the name of this function on Twitter. On Twitter and some other social networks, you can send a direct message only to a user who follows you.

Embed Code: An HTML code that allows photo or a video to be piped in from another site for viewing. Embed codes are best known for enabling the sharing of YouTube videos.

Fans: Users on Facebook who Like a company or group page. Once they Like your page, your content appears in their newsfeed, although exactly how often depends on Facebook's algorithm. Facebook no longer uses the term "fans" as a metric; it has since replaced it with "Likes." For example, a company who once had 2 million fans of its Facebook page now has 2 million Likes. However, many social practitioners still refer to their users as fans.

Favorite: Twitter's version of a "Like" for a given tweet.

Followers: Twitter's version of Facebook's friends. "Followers" hints at the asymmetric nature of Twitter relationships. Following Twitter users doesn't require their permission, and doesn't automatically sign them up for your own feed. Someone you follow has to choose to follow you to receive your posts in their feed, and for you to direct message them.

Follow Friday: Every Friday on Twitter, users show their fellow tweeters love by making suggestions the hashtag #ff. So for example, tweet "#ff @PeterFriedman @LiveWorld" on a Friday to encourage your readers to follow those accounts. (Why not?)

Forums: A website feature in which users can have asynchronous conversations by posting comments to the site. Comments are usually organized by topic, often in a hierarchical model called *threads.* Forums have been around since the earliest days of online community and the social web. They continue to be a popular feature of community sites and knowledge bases, and are sometimes used in a simple format on large social networks.

Friends: According to Facebook's own definition, people whom you have met in the "real world" before connecting on Facebook. However, with the rise of social networks, many people, especially those born after 1978, often first meet people online, become friends, and then meet offline.

Geotagging: Location-based tagging of content, enabling search based on location. For example, Instagram allows you to geotag to identify where your photo was taken. Posts on Facebook can be geotagged by default, if you choose.

Greenwashing: A critical term used to suggest that a company's cause campaign is more about improving brand image than about creating purposeful social change, and may not be representative of the company's true values or overall social impact. Often this view is inaccurate, and warrants a proactive social media effort to correct.

Hangout: A video feature offered on Google+ that allows unlimited users to watch a real-time video chat, with up to 10 users participating in the interactive chat. Hangouts can be recorded for distributing later.

Hashtag: A user-created tag that allows for search and discovery. Hashtags are frequently used to identify tweets related to conferences or events, or to create conversation threads around particular topics or social campaigns. Hashtags were first popularized on Twitter and are now spreading to Facebook and other social networks. They are even now used colloquially by people in texts, labels for photos, and everyday verbal language.

Like: An action Facebook users take by clicking the Like button to register and share their approval of a status update, or to subscribe to a company's page.

Listicle: An article in the form of a list. Typically those popular in the social web include animated GIFs and are often played for humor.

Location-Based Apps: Social applications that allow friends to announce their physical location to others in the network and build recognition based on the frequency of their visits to a particular locale. The most famous of these is FourSquare.

Lurker: Someone who participates passively in social spaces, reading, watching, and listening, but not commenting or taking any public actions. The vast majority of social community members and blog readers are for the most part lurkers; typically 10 percent of users, even in the most successful communities, are doing most of the interacting.

Meme: An idea, joke, or concept that resonates broadly and travels quickly online, often providing structure for individuals to add their own creativity to the theme. For example, a photo of Keanu Reeves sitting on a bench with a sad face sparked the "Sad Keanu" meme, in which users photoshopped his body from that image into hundreds of humorous scenarios.

Microblogging Platforms: Social platforms, most famously Tumblr, that encourage shorter posts than those on traditional blogs. Twitter is also often referred to as a microblogging channel.

Microvideo: Short social video, first popularized by Vine (acquired by Twitter), and now available on Instagram (acquired by Facebook). Vine videos are limited to 6 seconds; Instagram tops out at 15 seconds.

Moderation: Social spaces require tending to ensure that conversations and the overall environment create a positive experience for fans and community members. The tending of social spaces is especially important for big brands, allowing them to set the tone of the environment as well as mitigate the risk that negative or inappropriate comments could damage the brand or offend customers. Moderation (as opposed to monitoring) specifically involves the ability to take action on the content—approving, rejecting, and/or escalating it. Although there are some forms of automated moderation, only human moderators are able to evaluate posts with full sensitivity to context, nuance, and intent.

Monitoring: Monitoring (as opposed to moderation) involves reviewing content on the social web but taking no or limited action on it. Usually monitoring is applied in the context of listening and research to learn when a brand's name is used on the social web, evaluate the assorted content and conversations, and then analyze them. Sometimes monitoring leads to "escalating" the content to inform others about it. Moderation is a superset of monitoring that additionally can include approving, rejecting, escalating, and responding to content.

Newsfeed: The rolling aggregation of all the incoming news from members of your social network. On both Facebook and Twitter, the newsfeed is the centerpiece of the home page.

Newsreader: An application that allows readers to create their own central dashboard to aggregate their favorite blogs and online publications. Newsreaders have decreased in popularity as many publications now push their content through the major social channels. Popular examples include Flipboard and Feedly.

Podcast: A recorded audio broadcast that is distributed online, usually for free as a promotional tool or to build a community of enthusiasts. iTunes offers one of the most popular podcast distribution points.

Reach: As defined by Facebook, the number of unique people who saw an ad or post with social information. For example, if three people see an ad or post two times, each view indicating that a friend likes your Page, it counts as a social reach of three.

Retweet: A shared tweet on Twitter. Users have the option of "retweeting" to share a post with their followers.

Screencast: A video that captures action taking place on a computer screen, usually with audio narration. These are most frequently seen as explainer videos to show users how to use new site features or applications.

Sentiment: An analysis of the attitude of user comments, used to get a deeper read on whether interaction with users represents positive engagement. There are several tools available to measure sentiment, but as one participant in Live-World's South by Southwest workshop put it, "They're a crapshoot." Again, it's hard to replace human sensitivity.

Social Bookmarking: Applications that allows users to create and share bookmarks for webpages. The most well-known social bookmarking service is Delicious, founded in 2003.

Social Brand Identity: Follows on your overall brand identity, extending it to establish how customers will experience the brand through dialogue and relationships in the context of social media.

Socialized Brand: Has social at its core and woven through the entire brand experience, establishing the cultural context in which customers experience the brand through dialogue and relationships.

Story: Facebook terminology to refer to what users create when they make a post, or any time they interact with a brand's page. For example, commenting on a post or Liking one, claiming an offer, tagging the page in a photo, sharing a post, or any other of a number of social actions creates a story in their newsfeed. The number of stories your fans create adds up to the "Talking about this" metric.

Tag: Keywords added to a piece of content by users or in back-end analysis of content to help make it searchable. In Twitter, hashtags function as tags.

Tag Cloud: A visual aggregation of tags to show the content of websites, with the size of each tag representing the quantity of posts with that tag.

Talking About: The actual number of people who are "engaged" and interacting with a given page; in other words, the people who actually come back to the page beyond their initial Like action. This includes such activities as comments, Likes to a post, and shares by visitors to the page.

Terms of Service: The conditions users must accept and agree to when participating in your social spaces.

Timeline: What Facebook calls its profile page feature, the place where you "tell your life story through photos, friendships and personal milestones like graduating or traveling to new places."

Troll: Someone who regularly creates conflict and leaves negative comments in social spaces. Sometimes it's appropriate to ban users who are ruining the experience for everyone else.

Tweet: A post on Twitter.

Tweetup: A live event on Twitter. A Twitter user sets a date and time for followers to have a live, real-time discussion on a topic or topics of the host's choosing.

UGC (User-Generated Content): Any content created by users in social spaces.

Virality: Potential for exponential audience growth.

Webinar: Also referred to as a webcast, a live multimedia event, usually with interactive social features during the presentation. Webinar recordings are often shared after the fact to expand the audience for the content presentation.

Widgets: Portable applications that you can embed in websites, social channels, or apps to create new features or functionality.

Wiki: A collaborative knowledge base that allows anyone with access to create or edit content.

CPSIA information can be obtained at www.ICGtesting.com
Printed in the USA
BVOW08*2322140916

462151BV00001B/1/P